NEOCLASSICISM AND BIEDERMEIER

LIECHTENSTEIN MUSEUM VIENNA

NEOCLASSICISM AND BIEDERMEIER

Johann Kräftner
Academic assistant Stefan Körner

LIECHTENSTEIN M U S E U M

PRESTEL
Munich · Berlin · London · New York

CONTENTS

FOREWORD

In addition to numerous other valuable holdings, the Collections of the Prince of Liechtenstein, which count among the world's great private collections, contain a great number of paintings, works of sculpture and pieces of furniture dating from one of the most prolific and stylistically confident eras in Viennese art history – the period of the late eighteenth and early nineteenth centuries associated with two interconnected movements, Neoclassicism and Biedermeier. As had already been the case in the preceding Baroque era, the House of Liechtenstein played an important part in the emergence and evolution of these artistic styles. Its members were both active and influential in initiating great architectural projects, in commissioning work from sculptors and painters, and in collecting art. Numerous Liechtenstein residences – both city palaces and rural manor houses – were built at this time, and there were many ambitious schemes of rebuilding, remodelling, or restoration. The architect Joseph Hardtmuth, who was appointed to oversee such projects, left hardly a single Baroque structure untouched: the initially Renaissance palace at Wilfersdorf, for example, already converted by Anton Ospel into an imposing Baroque summer residence, now acquired a new, Neoclassical interior, but forfeited three of its four wings in addition to a substantial porch.

Some of the most important undertakings of this period were great exercises in landscape gardening; and, here too, the House of Liechtenstein was one of the chief pioneers. The transformation of the Baroque garden in the Rossau was soon followed by the laying out of the enormous park between Lednice and Valtice, and in due course by the redesign of the Hinterbrühl and of the Liechtenstein estates in Hadersfeld and Greifenstein. Here, the princes were able to indulge their innate penchant for the breeding of plants and to cultivate this interest in the true sense of the term. Their enthusiasm for assembling the most diverse range of plants and seeds also soon issued in financial reward. A series of ponds was created; and with the excess earth the landscape was redesigned (this activity providing the otherwise largely unemployed local population with work during the winter months). Fish from the ponds, sold at markets in Vienna, provided a good income, at least as long as the Church was able to ensure general adherence to its obligation to fast, and so to abjure meat. The cultivation of plants and genetically engineered varieties play a significant role in the activities of the House of Liechtenstein to this day.

The rich holdings of the Princely Collections are in themselves witness to the sumptuous decoration required by the substantial urban and rural residences inhabited by a line of princes and their families. Many of the pictures either commissioned or acquired in the eighteenth and early nineteenth centuries are preserved in the frames designed to accommodate these works within a particular scheme of interior decoration. In this respect, they testify both to the style of decoration and to the cultivated way of life prevailing in refined settings that have themselves not survived. Among the most important of these was the Liechtenstein palace that once stood on Herrengasse, in those long-forgotten days a true hub of social life in Vienna. This was also the site of the legendary concert hall,

the Bösendorfersaal. In 1913, already scheduled for demolition, it hosted a final, memorable concert, with the Rosé Quartet. Even after the last note had sounded and the lights had been extinguished, not a single member of the audience moved; but even their sadness at the imminent demolition of the palace could not prevent its destruction. This 'world of yesterday' does, however, live on in the pictures, the works of sculpture, and the pieces of furniture that have survived, often as its only physical remnants. This adds greatly to their interest and value in the twenty-first century, and it accounts for their role as the focus of the inaugural exhibition of the LIECHTENSTEIN MUSEUM.

Here, they embody the rich and complex interweaving of our chief concerns: a celebration of one of the most fruitful periods in the history of Vienna, the artistic developments of that era, and the supportive collecting activity of the House of Liechtenstein since the sixteenth century. Through choice objects from the Collections, our display documents the role of members of the House of Liechtenstein as collectors responding to the lure of Antiquity, their importance as art patrons, and their success as art collectors. The fact that this success endures is persuasively attested through the inclusion of some dazzling recent acquisitions: these include pictures by Friedrich von Amerling, Ferdinand Georg Waldmüller, and Francesco Hayez in addition to matchless porcelain plaques by Joseph Nigg and individual tea and coffee services once in the Bloch-Bauer Collection.

Without a team of extremely efficient colleagues, it would not have been possible for me to organize such an exhibition in parallel with the enormous task of overseeing the return of the Princely Collections to the recently restored Palais Liechtenstein at Rossau. I am, therefore, especially grateful to Andrea Stockhammer, Curator of the Liechtenstein Collections, who not only assumed the task of writing the entries for the catalogue of the permanent display, but also took on a great deal of other work in connection with the present publication. The fact that her colleague, Stefan Körner, was able, in the midst of such hectic activity, to discover as important a document as the original ground plan for the pyramid on the Anninger is more than gratifying. The commitment and adaptability of our publisher, Prestel Verlag, made it possible to incorporate up-to-the-minute information on such a find, in addition to a photographic record of the newly installed display rooms. I should like to express my particular thanks to my assistant, Alexandra Hanzl. Her creativity and her command of a difficult situation have allowed me the luxury of concentrating my energies on preparing the exhibition; her own involvement in this project has, moreover, helped me to realize as nearly as possible my vision of a truly great LIECHTENSTEIN MUSEUM.

For permitting me to realize this vision I am, of course, above all indebted to Prince Hans-Adam II and Princess Marie von und zu Liechtenstein and their family. As our exhibition makes very clear, the gratitude of Vienna, of Austria, and of art lovers everywhere is also due to these outstanding patrons.

Johann Kräftner
Director, LIECHTENSTEIN MUSEUM

INTRODUCTION

FOR DUTY AND FOR PLEASURE

ARCHITECTURAL PROJECTS IN VIENNA, LOWER AUSTRIA, AND MORAVIA UNDER ALOIS I AND JOHANN I VON LIECHTENSTEIN

Rarely has the broad spectrum of architectural projects of a particular period in history been so well illustrated by the achievements of a single family as is the case with those undertaken by the House of Liechtenstein between the late eighteenth and the first third of the nineteenth centuries. In the preceding era, the Baroque period, members of the Liechtenstein family seemed already to have realised every kind of building project: an abundance of new, or at least modernised, city palaces and rural manor houses appeared across their estates in the northern part of Lower Austria, in Moravia, and in Bohemia. Some of these were revolutionary structures designed to serve practical purposes, but there were also numerous others built purely for the pleasure of those commissioning them; here architects could give full vent to their imagination. In the Liechtenstein estates in Moravia manor houses sprung up, one after another, like pearls being threaded on a string. It seemed as if the members of the House of Liechtenstein were driven by the sheer joy of building, by an architecturally focused lust for collecting that had no basis in any real necessity.

Repeatedly, however, the truly progressive element in each phase of building activity soon degenerated into the merely conventional. It is, then, hardly surprising that a variety of factors – new intellectual and stylistic currents, new forms of economic organisation, new ways of perceiving nature, even simply the desire to keep up with the latest trends – spurred the architects employed, as the willing tools of their respective masters, to ever new *tours de force*. In no time at all new buildings and schemes of modernisation would be underway.

Becoming increasingly mobile at this period, the wealthy sought to match their surroundings to the time of year; and, more than ever before, they created environments to facilitate this luxury. When it was cold they would remain within the thick walls of their old city palaces; but during the hot summers, as well as in autumn with its socially crucial hunting season, they moved to the country, to their manor houses. Nonetheless, for the Liechtensteins, as for other noble families, Vienna remained the focus of their chief concerns and social obligations, as well as the place from which their estates could best be administered. As one would therefore expect, their first great architectural project of the post-Baroque period was realised in the city.

Within walking distance of the Majoratspalais (the residence traditionally reserved for the eldest son and heir) in Bankgasse, there already stood a palace in the Herrengasse in the Baroque style. On the orders of Alois I von Liechtenstein (1759–1805), this was modernised and, in the process, annexed to the neighbouring buildings to create a single, sprawling complex. This was intended to meet both administration (it included a suite of offices as well as stables, a riding school, and a library) and residential needs.

The reconstruction of the palace in Herrengasse was commissioned in 1788 from Joseph Meissl the Elder (1758–90), who had at that point been employed for a year as architect to the prince. After Meissl's death, this position passed to his nephew, Joseph Hardtmuth (1758–1816), who had collaborated on the scheme from the start. Under Hardtmuth, the project was brought to completion in 1792, apparently to the prince's complete satisfaction. In both the articulation of its exterior and the arrangement of its sequences of rooms, the palace in its new guise constituted a persuasive image of the power and importance of the House of Liechtenstein. Hardtmuth's architecture had an emphatic and spirited 'signature', an assertive confidence. In both interior and exterior he played with the alignment of paired columns and the impression of power that these inevitably conveyed – a stylistic device that may well have ensured the architectonic impact of the building on what was a difficult site in the narrow Herrengasse. The reserved elegance of the architecture and interiors associated with the reign of the Emperor Josef I (r. 1780–90), epitomised by the

< **JOHANN ZIEGLER, ENGRAVED AFTER LORENZ JANSCHA**
Roman Ruins in Schönbrunn Park
Dedicated to Prince Alois I von Liechtenstein
Engraving, coloured, 1782

WILHELM J. BURGER
Façade of the Liechtenstein palace in Herrengasse,
by Joseph Hardtmuth (built 1788–92)
Photo, *c.* 1910

JOSEPH HARDTMUTH
Ground-floor plan of the Liechtenstein Chancellery
in Herrengasse and adjacent Tax House
In the courtyard, the already extant Riding School.
Pen on pencil on paper, with wash, immediately post-1790

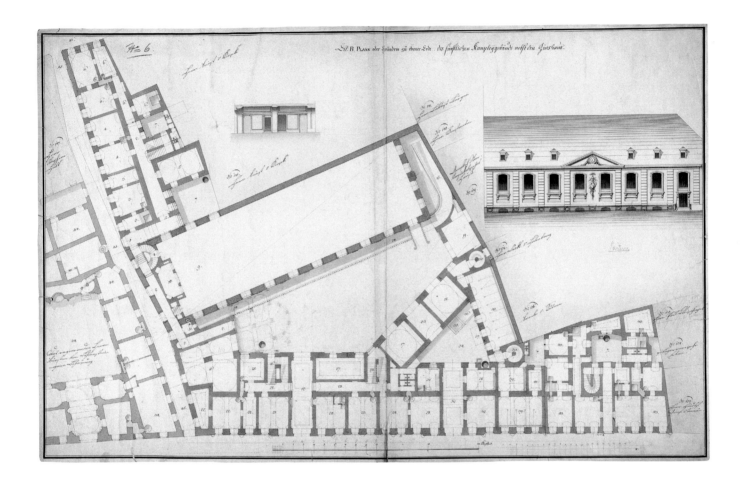

Josephinum library built in 1783–85 by Isidore Ganneval (1730–86), was altogether renounced in Hardtmuth's own generously expansive three-bay library hall, which offered an emphatic, almost imperial affirmation of princeliness. This outcome was certainly assisted by the use of colour: the yellow of the columns harmonises with the green and gold of the furnishings, which Hardtmuth deliberately incorporated within his overall scheme of decoration.

Comparison with other Viennese libraries of this period reveals the substantial scale of this one, and this in turn hints at the pretensions it was required to satisfy. With its holdings of around 40,000 volumes, it was one of the largest collections of its kind in the city, surpassed only by the Imperial Court Library (Hofbibliothek), the University Library and

the private library of the Austrian Emperor Franz I (r. 1792–1835). The residential quarters were of a corresponding opulence; but the original articulation of the walls with pilasters and intervening compartments was soon redesigned in the bourgeois Biedermeier style, which was prevalent in Austria and Germany from 1815 to 1860 and featured Neoclassical, Empire, and Regency elements. A detailed impression of the original appearance of the library and of many other interiors is now only to be had through records made before this was altered: there are, for example, watercolours from the second half of the 1830s, mostly by Rudolf von Alt (1812–1905), as well as photographs. Further indispensable aspects of aristocratic life and the need to uphold status, as these were perceived at the time of the planning and

JOSEPH HARDTMUTH
Façade of the Liechtenstein palace
in Herrengasse (built 1788–92)
Pen on pencil on paper, 1790

erection of the palace, were accommodated by the Riding School and the stables. These were located on the two floors below the library: the stables at ground level, the Riding School above them. Prince Johann I von Liechtenstein (1760–1836) was a keen rider and is said to have made a habit of breaking in horses daily, after breakfast; and sixty to eighty of these noble animals were at all times available to this end in his stables. How rapidly this way of life changed under his successor, Alois II (himself President of the Viennese horse racing society), is attested in the fact that, as early as 1837, the palace in Herrengasse was rented out to the Russian Ambassador to Vienna, Count Tatischeff, and from 1845 to various state employees and to a number of private individuals.

The possession of property was increasingly valued as a source of income, and one house after another would be rented out or even sold. In 1872 the Riding School gave way to a celebrated concert hall, the Bösendorfersaal: seating 588, this remained the centre of musical life in Vienna until it was demolished in 1913. Stefan Zweig, in his memoirs, *Die Welt von Gestern* (The World of Yesterday), recalls the

last concert to be held there: the music played by the Rose Quartet, the candles that were slowly extinguished, and the audience who remained seated in the hall after the lights had been extinguished, in order to hold back the passage of time, at least for a few more minutes. After the site had remained unused for two decades, the first skyscraper in Vienna was erected there in 1933.

Of the palace that once stood in Herrengasse, sold in 1913 and itself eventually demolished, only some of the furniture and decoration has been preserved. Most notably, the furniture and fittings of the library were, in 1913, adapted to a new setting, the Garden Palace (Gartenpalais) at Rossau, where they can be admired by the public to this day. There also remain a few sections of the wall panelling; and, in the light of both the frames of the pictures (specially designed for this decorative scheme) and a number of surviving chandeliers, we can draw our own conclusions as to the quality of this unique ensemble. The building taking place in Vienna was, however, only one tiny aspect of the broad palette of architectural activity going on throughout the Liechtenstein estates. In Moravia Joseph Hardtmuth had reconstructed

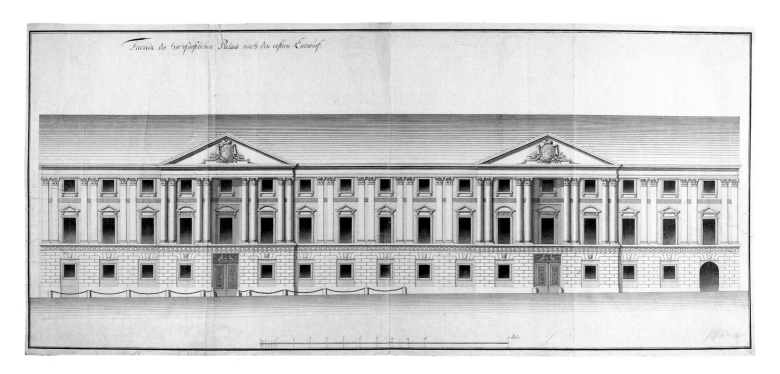

JOSEPH HARDTMUTH
Façade of the Liechtenstein palace
in Herrengasse (built 1788–92)
Pen on pencil on paper, with wash, 1790 (detail)

JOSEPH HARDTMUTH

Cross-section of stables, Riding School and library
(built 1791) of the Liechtenstein palace in Herrengasse
Pen on pencil on paper, with wash, *c.* 1790

JOSEPH HARDTMUTH

Cross-section of stairwell of the Liechtenstein palace
in Herrengasse (built 1788–92)
Pen on pencil on paper, with wash, *c.* 1790

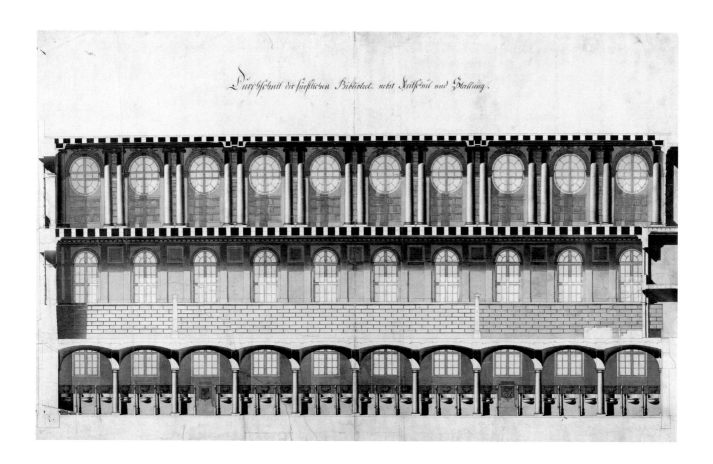

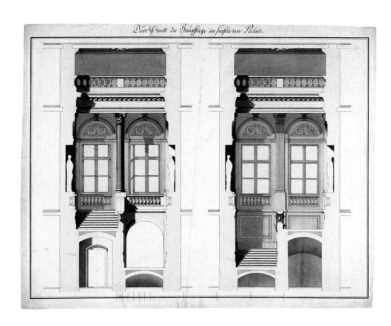

WILHELM J. BURGER
View of main aisle of the library (built 1791) of the Liechtenstein palace
in Herrengasse, by Joseph Hardtmuth (built 1788–92)
Photo *c.* 1910

RUDOLF VON ALT
Bedroom next to the Winter Garden of the Liechtenstein palace
in Herrengasse, by Joseph Hardtmuth
(built 1788–92, Winter Garden 1805–08)
Watercolour, 1837

RUDOLF VON ALT
Study at the Liechtenstein palace
in Herrengasse, by Joseph Hardtmuth
(built 1788–92)
Watercolour, 1837

JOSEPH HARDTMUTH

Drawing of gateway to the *cour d'honneur* of the Liechtenstein
Garden Palace with the still untruncated stable wings.
Pen on pencil on paper, with wash, 1793

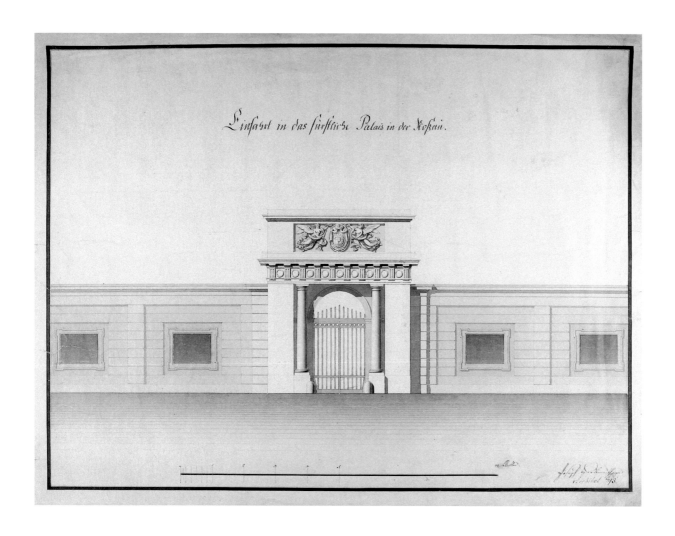

JOSEPH KORNHÄUSEL

Drawing of gateway to the *cour d'honneur* of the Liechtenstein Garden Palace.
The stable wings have been replaced by a fence, the coat of arms by an inscription.
Pen on pencil on paper, with wash, 1814

JOSEPH HARDTMUTH
Drawing of the Trajan Column on the Anninger
near Mödling (built 1811)
Pen on pencil on paper, with wash, 1811

JOSEPH HARDTMUTH
Drawing of the pyramid on the Anninger near Mödling,
ground plan
Pen on pencil on paper, with wash, 1811

a great many pre-existent palaces and manor houses; others were
built from scratch. From 1806 he carried out important adaptations at
Eisgrub; in the years 1805–08, he devised both the reconstruction
of a manor house at Mährisch-Aussee, near Littau, on the site of an
earlier building by Antonio Beduzzi, which had been destroyed by fire
and, around the same time, from 1806 to 1808, was responsible for
another new building, Adamsthal manor house, near Brno. All of these,
in as far as they survive, are distinguished by a somewhat unorthodox
approach to the architectural vocabulary of Classicism and by an
almost forbidding heaviness and sobriety.

Hardtmuth, however, devoted himself not only to the creation of such
grand buildings, but also – and arguably in an even more fruitful fashion – to the erection of smaller, and formally more consequential,
structures intended purely to delight his patron (the so-called volup-
tuary buildings), which sprung up in astonishing numbers. Most of
these were built close to the confluence of the Thaya and March rivers,
between Feldsberg, Eisgrub, and Lundenburg, an area that was transformed into expansive, English-style parklands; and they were also to
be found in the Brühl. This was the original family seat of the Liechtensteins, who in 1807 were able to buy it back from Prince Stanislaus
Poniatowsky, and ultimately to transform it into a castle in the Romantic style. Building was also carried out along the shores of the River
Danube, between Hadersfeld and Greifenstein (properties acquired in
1776 and 1807, respectively), and at the aforementioned Adamsthal,
near Brno, not far from the large ironworks owned by the Liechtenstein family.

In every case, the surrounding landscape was transformed into a
series of areas for relaxation, interspersed with points affording exceptionally good views; and there would be small hunting lodges and monuments built in memory of a particular person or event. The smallest
incidents might be deemed reason enough to erect some form of
memorial, and these would also serve as objects of aesthetic pleasure. Hardtmuth took his models from among the Neoclassical motifs
to be found in the history of architecture – the obelisk, the colonnade,
the triumphal arch – and freely re-worked and combined these into
something new.

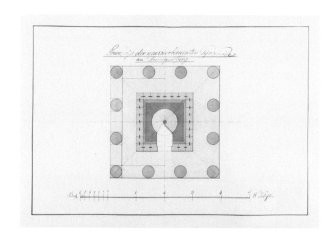

JOSEPH HARDTMUTH

Drawing of the pyramid on the Anninger near Mödling,
view and section
Pen on pencil on paper, with wash, 1811

FERDINAND RUNK
View of the Turkish Tower in the park at Eisgrub (Lednice),
by Joseph Hardtmuth (built 1797–1804)
Gouache, *c.* 1825

Turkish Tower in the park at Eisgrub (Lednice), by Joseph Hardtmuth
(built 1797–1804)

Even in the context of Hardtmuth's work, his designs for the *Pyramid* and for the *Trajan Column* are unequalled in their architectonic radicalism; and the strereometric clarity in the interconnection of their distinct elements was clearly influenced by the extreme form of Neoclassicism associated with the French Revolution. The *Trajan Column* stood on a hill at the Anninger near Mödling, but collapsed in 1811 shortly after construction had commenced. He designed the pyramid to replace it, but Hardtmuth's project of 1811 was rejected by Prince Johann I and Hardtmuth consequently lost his post as architect to the prince.

Architecturally the pyramid is related to the Turkish tower (or 'mosque') at Eisgrub. Viewed from the terrace of the manor house at Eisgrub, built from 1797 to 1804, this structure evinces a similar evolution in its architectural elements, and its minaret rises to sixty-eight metres from an encased, rectangular, two-storey base.

JOSEPH HARDTMUTH
Drawing of Campo Formio obelisk in the avenue
to Prittlach (Pritluky) near Eisgrub (Lednice) (built 1798)
Pen on pencil on paper, with wash, 1798

Campo Formio obelisk in the avenue to Prittlach (Pritluky)
near Eisgrub (Lednice), by Joseph Hardtmuth (built 1798)

Colonnade on Reistenberg near Feldsberg (Valtice),
by Joseph Hardtmuth (built 1810–12, completed by
Joseph Kornhäusel)

The obelisk, as a vertical element projecting from the open landscape, exerted a particular fascination in this period. In Hardtmuth's work we encounter it repeatedly. In 1796, between Eisgrub and the neighbouring settlement of Pittlach, Prince Alois I had a double row of trees planted, four kilometres long and seventeen metres wide, and in 1798 Hardtmuth placed at one extremity, as a monument to the Peace of Campo Formio, an obelisk that stands to this day.

In 1810–11, in the Hinterbrühl, not far from the remains of the ancestral seat of the Liechtensteins, Hardtmuth erected the ruin of an amphitheatre, constructed out of rough, almost unhewn blocks of stone. Here, too, as in the design for the pyramid, the arcades were supported on stone columns without capitals. In Feldsberg, in 1810–12, on the hill on which the architect Johann Bernhard Fischer von Erlach had probably planned to build a manor house for himself,

Colonnnade on Reistenberg near Feldsberg (Valtice),
by Joseph Hardtmuth (built 1810–12)

FERDINAND RUNK
Colonnade near the Adamsthal Manner House,
by Joseph Hardtmuth (built *c.* 1808)
Gouache, *c.* 1825

Hardtmuth combined a colonnade (that is to say, an unarched row of columns) and a triumphal arch, which is deftly hidden at its centre. The site was dedicated to the memory of the prince's father and brothers. A further colonnade was erected at Adamsthal, on this occasion a simpler structure, conceived as a ruin. For his Temple of Diana in Feldsberg (also built in 1810–12), Hardtmuth again took the motif of the tripartite triumphal arch of Classical Antiquity, as found in the Arch of

Constantine in Rome, but reduced it to a single-arch arrangement, thereby uniting the familiar with the new. Beneath its roof he placed a large hall intended for hunting parties.

In addition to serving the prince's pleasure, Hardtmuth was also responsible for meeting all his patron's requirements with regard to structures that had a practical purpose: from the large stud farm that he devised for Hohenau (1803), by way of the show farm at the new

Pohansko Hunting Lodge near Lundenburg (Breclav), by Joseph Hardtmuth
(built 1810–12, completed by Joseph Kornhäusel)
Photo, *c.* 1930

manor house in Feldsberg (1809–10; this in fact served both for the
breeding of horses and for princely pleasure), to a small sheep-shed,
a mustard factory and a mill. Each of these, albeit not designed by
Hardtmuth himself, nonetheless required his consent before building
work could commence. And there are, indeed, numerous records of
his closer involvement in such minor projects.

RUDOLF VON ALT
View over swan lake at Schloss Eisgrub (Lednice)
before being rebuildt in 1845
Watercolour, *c.* 1830

FERDINAND RUNK
View of the Renaissance castle at Lundenburg,
turned by Joseph Hardtmuth into an artificial ruin
Gouache, *c.* 1825

JOSEPH KLIEBER
Relief on the Temple of Diana in Theimwald near Feldsberg
(Valtice) by Joseph Hardtmuth (built 1810–12, completed
by Joseph Kornhäusel)

FERDINAND RUNK
Temple of Diana in Theimwald near Feldsberg, by Joseph
Hardtmuth (1810–12, completed by Joseph Kornhäusel)
Gouache, *c.* 1820

FERDINAND RUNK
View of the Amphitheatre and Manor House by Franz Engel
(built 1820–22) and the Still Ruinous Liechtenstein Castle
near Maria Enzersdorf
Gouache, *c.* 1820

In view of the numerous roles that Hardtmuth fulfilled as architect to the prince, and the degree of commitment that he also brought to his independent activity as both inventor and manufacturer (it is to him that we owe the sort of ceramic lead that we still use in pencils and in modern earthenware), it is not surprising that there were also a great many oversights, some of them resulting in calamity (not least, the previously mentioned collapse of the Trajan Column on the Anninger during construction work in 1811 and the Hussars' Temple there the following year during a storm). The patience and confidence of the prince notwithstanding, Hardtmuth's contract was terminated on 1 April 1812.

ANONYMOUS

View of the Hussars Temple on the Kleiner Anninger
near Mödling, by Joseph Kornhäusel (built 1812)
Watercolour on pencil and pen on paper, *c.* 1820

JOSEPH KORNHÄUSEL

Working drawing for the Hussars' Temple
on the Kleiner Anninger near Mödling (built 1812)
Pen on pencil on paper, with wash, 1812

View of Entrance Hall and Main Façade of the Hunting Lodge in
Katzelsdorf Forest near Feldsberg (Valtice), by Joseph Kornhäusel
(built 1818–19)
Photos, *c.* 1925

View of the Rear and Front of the Temple of Apollo by the Mill
Pool near Lundenburg (Breclav), by Joseph Kornhäusel
(built 1818–19)
Photos, *c.* 1925

View of the Front of the Lake Pavilion on the Middle Lake
at Eisgrub (Lednice), by Joseph Kornhäusel (built 1814–16)
Photo, *c.* 1925

Within the same year Joseph Kornhäusel (1782–1860) was appointed Hardtmuth's successor. To begin with, he completed Hardtmuth's brilliant designs for the small hunting lodge at Pohansko near Lundenburg (1810–12), and the Temple of Diana and the colonnade in Feldsberg. Thereafter, however, his output altered considerably as he moved away from Hardtmuth's imposing, voluminous, Neoclassical heaviness towards the carefree, bucolic lightness of Biedermeier. And the commissions that Kornhäusel now received were themselves of a different character. The Liechtensteins no longer required large metropolitan or rural residences; their desire was, above all, for small, refined structures designed for the pursuit of pleasure and deftly integrated into the setting of a park. And it was in this genre that Kornhäusel established himself as the great master of the new era. The palace on the lake of 1814–16, the hunting lodge in Katzelsdorf Forest of 1818–19, and the Temple of Apollo of 1818–19 are Kornhäusel's masterpieces. Perfectly aligned with the trajectory of the sun during the course of the day, they were incorporated into the Arcadian, pond-dotted landscape between Eisgrub and Feldsberg.

In Vienna, meanwhile, in the immediate proximity of his planned *Bach Circus* (1807–08), Kornhäusel completed for the Liechtensteins the ensemble of buildings on the Schüttel in the Prater district through the addition of a new pleasure palace (1814–16), the design in fact constituting an early form of the nineteenth-century villa and testifying to the general shift, in the history of architectural taste, from a monumental bulkiness to French-inspired elegance. Sadly, our knowledge of what must have been a structure of immense charm comes only from plans and views; by 1839 this influential prototype was already being rented out, and in 1910 it was demolished.

However, like his predecessor, Kornhäusel was not able to dwell uninterruptedly on the upper slopes of the Olympus of architecture; he, too, was burdened with commissions at the other end of the spectrum – as demonstrated by his design for a modest sheep-shed. And perhaps for Kornhäusel, too, this sort of working relationship with a single patron proved too trying: ultimately, the two quarrelled, and this led, in 1818, to a parting of ways.

Kornhäusel's successor, the prolific Franz Engel (1776–1827), continued building in very much the same, light spirit. Engel was responsible for extensive projects, such as the rebuilding of a Baroque manor house below the ruins in the Hinterbrühl (1820–22), but also for a series of small pleasure palaces, above all for the Liechtenstein estates in southern Moravia. Nonetheless, for all the charm and sensi-

tivity with which Engel was able to incorporate his structures into their landscape settings, the buildings themselves invariably strike us now as a little too worthy. This is the case, for example, with the *Circus of the Three Graces in Feldsberg* (1825), which was intended to enclose a group of figures of 1790 by Johann Martin Fischer (1740–1820), transferred from elsewhere in the same park. It is also true of the so-called Grenzschloss, or 'manor house on the border', of 1826–27 (completed by Josef Poppelak), aligned in relation to the rising sun and standing on the western shore of the large pond called Nimmersatt, between Feldsberg and Eisgrub, on the border between Lower Austria and Moravia.

Nearby lay the source of a spring, gushing from an urn held by a nymph, and it was this stream that flowed through the arcade of the central hall of Engel's building into the pond lying in front of it. This rather more literary inspiration than we find in the case of perhaps any other building testifies to the tendency of Biedermeier towards reverie and the sense of an intimate connection with nature and landscape. In a watercolour of 1839, Joseph Höger (who was employed by the prince as a drawing teacher for his children) shows the dreamy view of the central hall, rendered in pale violet tones, with its celebrated Neoclassical vase above the pond, where we find a boat rocking to and fro in the gentle waves. In a preliminary version of his design, Engel clearly modelled his scheme on the architecture of the Middle Ages, and he placed a small ruined castle on the bank of the pond, linking the two parts of the manor house (one on the Austrian and the other on the Moravian side of the border) by means of a wooden bridge – a solution that the prince rejected. In his final but in fact more awkward design, Engel had apparently been thinking of Hardtmuth's *Hansenburg* near Eisgrub (1807–10), which employed Gothic forms, in particular grisaille wall paintings in its interior. But Engel also seems to anticipate the emerging vogue for Romantic Historicism, whose origins can partly be traced to such examples of parkland architecture.

Despite the repeated evidence of the fertility of Engel's imagination and the *joie de vivre* that his buildings convey – his palace theatre at Eisgrub was regarded as the finest of its kind to be found in the Austro-Hungarian Monarchy – his architecture can seem rather dry. This would certainly be true of his *Liechtenstein Mausoleum in Wranau*, near Brno (1819–21; which owes its distinction to its sculptural component, provided by Klieber) and, above all, of his manor house in the Hinterbrühl. The effective *reductio ad absurdum* in this decline is to be found in the unexecuted and undated plan of the early 1820s for a gigantic

FERDINAND RUNK
View of the Liechtenstein Pleasure Palace on the Schüttel
in the Prater, Vienna, with its Stables on the Left
by Joseph Kornhäusel (built 1814–16)
Gouache, *c.* 1825

Liechtenstein mansion on a site that lay at the entrance to the Jäger-zeile (Praterstrasse) in the Leopoldstadt district of Vienna. If erected, this would have been out of all proportion to the buildings in its vicinity, and would have resembled an ocean-going ship stranded in the Danube Canal. On these grounds alone, the scheme was bound to fail.

The architecture of the Biedermeier Era reached its perfection in small structures. Even Kornhäusel failed in his attempts to work on a grand scale – with one truly masterly exception: the Weilburg in Baden near Vienna (1820–23). Large-scale projects therefore generally eluded

him, as in the case of the competition of 1828–31 for a new building to house the Parliament of Lower Austria. Engel's unexecuted design, with its failure to manipulate or give meaning to oversized structural masses, graphically illustrates the end of Biedermeier architecture. By this date both the scale of the commission and the way it was interpreted were already a thing of the past. Like the architect himself, the scheme was simply too far removed from reality. In 1827 Engel died in Dr Görgen's insane asylum in Vienna, to which he had been admitted two years earlier.

JOSEPH HÖGER
View of the Grenzschloss on Bischofwart Pond
by Franz Engel (built 1826–27)
Watercolour, 1839

View of the Grenzschloss on Bischofwart Pond

FRANZ ENGEL

Drawing for a Liechtenstein palace on the Danube Canal in Vienna,
showing the entrance façade, ground plan and Danube front
Pen on pencil on paper, with wash, early 1820s

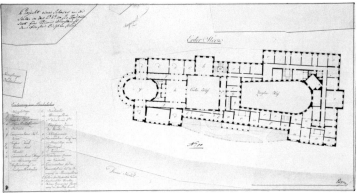

GALLERY I

THE RISE OF INTEREST IN ANTIQUITY

The subject of this first section of the display is Rome, the Rome of the ruins of Antiquity, ruins that simply lay about on the ground; the Rome that, during the Renaissance, was resurrected in the imagination of writers and artists; and, ultimately, the Rome that, in the seventeenth and eighteenth centuries, became the treasured model, the source of inspiration and the trend-setter for the latest movements in art and architecture.

It was in Rome that Antiquity was best understood and, indeed, directly experienced. Even after the devastation wrought by the era of mass migrations and then by the Sack of Rome in 1527, the city's inhabitants continued to live among its ruins. Here, in what remained of the former centre of the world (which was soon to assume something of its old importance), one could find patrician families comfortably installed in their medieval towers as well as more modestly but no less happily housed citizens. With apparently few hesitations, not only were the ancient building types and models of Rome appropriated, but so too were the building materials themselves – be it for structural needs or for decorative purposes. In continuing this well-established local practice, the Italian Renaissance both discovered the beauty of this bygone world and celebrated its 'rebirth' – the term that came to characterise the era as a whole.

In the early sixteenth century there arose an awareness of this extraordinary heritage and of its significance for the present. Pope Nicholas V (r. 1447–55) founded the Vatican Library, thereby providing the next generation with the foundations for their own interest in the Humanities and in Antiquity through the literature collected and translated under his auspices. Under Popes Julius II (r. 1503–13) and Leo X (r. 1513–21) great attention was paid to the acquisition of sculpture and to the discovery and conservation of the works of Antiquity. Artists and those with an interest in art started to explore the numerous ruins of Ancient Rome. The soil of Rome was blessed with precious statues, fragments of painted mural, and other works of art. In 1506 the owner of a vineyard came upon a subterranean vaulted chamber when digging up part of his own land and, preserved within it, a large and more or less undamaged sculpture that proved to be the Hellenistic figural group known as the *Laocoön*. Julius II appointed the artists Giuliano da Sangallo (1443–1516) and Michelangelo Buonarroti (1475–1564) to inspect and appraise the sculptural works that he had previously acquired and installed in the Vatican Belvedere. Among these were the pieces subsequently named after their location: the *Apollo Belvedere* and the *Belvedere Torso*.

Knowledge of such objects was rapidly disseminated by means of engravings and through the three-dimensional copies that were, of necessity, made as a substitute for the highly sought-after originals. In 1515 Leo X transferred responsibility for overseeing all new architectural and sculptural finds to another artist, the painter Raphael (1483–1520), who, in a celebrated letter, insisted on the importance of preserving all that had survived from Antiquity. Addressing both his predecessors and his contemporaries, he lamented: 'How many popes have demolished the temples, statues, arches and other splendid works of art of Antiquity! How many carved columns and ornaments have been transformed into mere chalk dust!'

These works of Antiquity were recognised as extremely precious. They were, accordingly, not accessible to everyone, but only to the Pope of the time and to the Roman nobility. These competed with unbridled zeal to lay claim to such evidence of the city's glorious past: for to possess one of these works was also to be assured of the greatest prestige. This re-emerging Ancient Rome was also captured in the sketches of celebrated artists, among them the Netherlandish painter Hermanus Posthumus (1513/14–88). His *Landscape with Roman Ruins*, executed in 1536, is one of the most delightful documents of this yearning for ruins. Only a short period of Posthumus's career has been securely traced: the years when he was employed, as 'Master Herman', by Duke Wilhelm IV of Bavaria (r. 1508–50), for whom he collaborated with others on providing decorations for the ducal residence in Landshut. It is only in the last few years that research has begun to throw light on the rest of his life.

Landshut was at this time closely associated with the ideas introduced by the Italian Renaissance, for it was in a corresponding style that the aforementioned Duke had his residence innovatively and expansively rebuilt. He had married a Gonzaga, which explains the proximity of his own tastes in art and architecture to those of the ducal court in Mantua and, furthermore, the possible collaboration in the work at Landshut of the Mantuan court artist Giulio Romano (c. 1499–1546). It would be fair to assume that Posthumus, too, had visited Mantua before 1540. In Landshut he worked on the decoration of the 'Italian Wing', where the chapel has an altarpiece bearing his signature. His possible other contributions to this section of the residence have yet to be established, but records of fees paid to him show that he must have played an important role in providing its decoration. It is possible that a sumptuous Renaissance chest, recently acquired for the Princely Collections, once formed part of the decorative programme.

HERMANUS POSTHUMUS *c.* 1513/14 – 88
Landscape with Roman Ruins, 1536
I.1

In his *Landscape with Roman Ruins*, Hermanus Posthumus depicts the discovery of the remains of Ancient Rome, a world at that date still largely unexplored and, consequently, full of mysteries and surprises. The precise knowledge of the ruins of Antiquity evinced in this picture strongly suggests that the artist himself had the opportunity to study the originals in Rome. In the foreground we can see the *Domus Aurea* (Emperor Nero's 'Golden House') with its elaborate painted decoration in a style that was soon to be known as 'grotesque'. This had been discovered around 1480, when excavations were carried out at a mound north of the Colosseum, and in the 1530s it was regarded as one of

the great attractions of the Eternal City. In one room of this former palace complex, known as the *volta nera*, some of the artists who had travelled to Rome, including a certain 'HEMSKERC' and a 'HER POSTA', had added their own contributions. Doubtless, these inscriptions are to be identified, respectively, with the Netherlandish painter Maerten van Heemskerck (1498–1574) and Hermanus Posthumus. In 1536, on the occasion of the triumphal entry into Rome of Emperor Karl V (1500–58), Posthumus was required to decorate the Porta San Sebastiano with a triumphal arch – there are records of the involvement in this project of a certain 'Maestro Ermanno'. It is possible that

he had encountered triumphal arches before his stay in Rome, having
come across them when in North Africa, where he and a fellow artist,
Jan Cornelisz. Vermeyen (c. 1500–59), had accompanied Karl V's
Tunisian Campaign.

Within his composition, Posthumus assembles buildings and sculptures
in an idealised northern European landscape. He affords a glimpse
into half-buried caves and shows us architects using triangle and com-
pass to measure and record the ruins before them. The explorers
plunged headlong into this landscape of ruins, for the first time truly
engaging with it. They discovered a new excitement in the devastation
that, since the decline of the culture of Antiquity, had been the barely
noticed setting for everyday life.

Posthumus invents fantastical architectural structures, but he also
appears to have carefully recorded what he observed. It has proved
possible to point to sixty-five specific structures (though not all are precisely identifiable) and to six examples of mural painting that seem to
have provided his visual sources. The massive head at the centre of
the picture is that of the *Juno Ludovisi*, acquired in 1622 by the Roman
family of that name and now on display in the city's Museo Nazionale
Romano. Also to be seen is an extravagant monument flanked by two
Egyptian lions made of basalt, which are now in the Vatican Museum.
Posthumus has, however, also rendered as a beautifully overgrown ruin
the mausoleum of the daughter of the Roman Emperor Constantine,
which in reality had been preserved almost intact, having been converted into the memorial church of Santa Costanza. Similarly, the *Torlonia
Vase*, installed in 1536 in the Cesi Gardens and recorded by Heemskerck as still all of a piece, is shown by Posthumus as broken into
several pieces.

The picture is inscribed with a centrally placed motto derived from
Ovid's *Metamorphoses*: 'TEMPVS EDAX RERVM TVQVE INVIDIOSA
VESTVSTAS O[MN]IA DESTRVITIS' (Oh, most voracious Time, and you,
envious Age, you destroy everything). Every human activity, we are
here both told and shown, is at the mercy of transience. When architects and artists measured and drew the ruins of Antiquity they were
also engaging in a vain battle with the evidence of transience and
decay. Somewhat like Sisyphus, they slaved away in order to preserve,
or at least pass on to posterity, the last of what had survived. Is this
perhaps a metaphor for the struggle of the artist, above all of Raphael,
who wanted to put a stop to the raids of the plunderers and specula-
tive builders, who in those days enthusiastically undertook to create a
new Rome?

BENVENUTO TISI, CALLED IL GAROFALO 1481–1559

The Apotheosis of Hercules, *c.* 1539

I.3

MAERTEN VAN HEEMSKERCK 1498–1574

Landscape with St Jerome, 1547

I.2

Like Hermanus Posthumus, Maerten van Heemskerck, who was in Rome from 1527 to 1532, was also a slave to this enchantment with Antiquity. He had caught the bug from his compatriot and friend, Jan van Scorel (1492–1562), who in 1524 had returned to Haarlem from a visit to Rome and had recounted his impressions to Heemskerck. It is possible that Posthumus had trained in the workshop of Jan van Scorel. The artistic proximity of Heemskerck and Posthumus is also demonstrated by the fact that an increasing number of drawings of Roman ruins formerly ascribed to Heemskerck have recently been attributed to Posthumus.

Heemskerck made an entire series of sketches recording this Rome of the 1530s in the process of upheaval, and he later combined these into *capricci* that took the form of large oil paintings. In his *Landscape with St Jerome* – the landscape itself was in fact later reworked, per-

haps by Jan Joest van Cossiau – he unfurls an expansive panorama strewn with ruins, yet he is only moderately interested in his ostensible protagonist. The saint crouches insignificantly at the left edge of the composition and is, as it were, only its pretext. Instead of the usual iconographic practice of locating this penitent in an imposing cave landscape in the desert, the artist places him in an urban wasteland, a metropolitan no man's land, familiar to us from photographs taken in the wake of wars or natural catastrophes. Heemskerck may have recalled that Jerome, after his period of atonement in the desert, was employed as secretary to Pope Damasus I (305–84) and, accordingly, re-located to the ruins of Rome.

Like Posthumus in his *Landscape with Roman Ruins*, Heemskerck sought to lend substance to the dream of the former greatness of Rome. The composition is in fact full of quotations testifying to

ANONYMOUS, BOLOGNESE
Bust of Flora, *c.* 1700
I.4

ANONYMOUS, FRENCH
Bust of the Dying Alexander, 2nd half of 17th century
I.5

MARCANTONIO FRANCESCHINI 1648–1729
Diana and Actaeon, 1692/98
I.6

Heemskerck's knowledge both of Antiquity and of contemporary building activity in Rome. Here, for example, we find fragments from the Temple of Saturn, the first temple to be built in the Forum Romanum, alongside a recessed pilaster with rich figurative decoration, this last being a quotation from Raphael's *School of Athens*, painted in 1509–11 for the Vatican Stanze della Segnatura, the Papal Law Courts. Beneath the arch Hercules and Antaeus are seen wrestling, just as they do in the model in the Vatican Belvedere, now part of the Vatican Museum. It was in the Belvedere that Heemskerck had also seen the large figure of the River Tiber, which he here deftly links with the Lupa Romana (the Roman she-wolf) and the twins she raised, Romulus and Remus. Also to be identified here are a fragment of the Colosseum, the stepped dome of the Pantheon, and Trajan's Column. The claim of the formal canon of Antiquity to eternal validity is here combined, in an entirely Mannerist spirit, with the notion of the tran-

sience of all the works of man: it is not certain which will survive. A completely different type of longing for Antiquity informs the large mural *Diana and Actaeon* painted by Marcantonio Franceschini (1648–1729). This is a fragment of the original decoration of the Garden Palace at Rossau commissioned by Johann Adam Andreas I von Liechtenstein (1657–1712), an image from the artist's Ovid series and originally intended to adorn an entire room, as a prototype for the overall decorative programme conceived by the prince. It was planned that the paintings should take up the full height of each of the rooms, in the manner of tapestries, and cover the walls in their entirety. Depicted is an episode from Ovid's *Metamorphoses* in which Actaeon, the young hunter, surprises the goddess Diana and her nymphs while they are bathing in a grotto – and is thereby doomed to die. Diana punishes Actaeon by turning him into a stag, who is then torn to pieces by his own dogs, these failing to recognise him in his new guise.

ANONYMOUS
Bust of Apollo, 18th century
I.7

GIUSEPPE PISANI 1757–1839
Bust of Zeus, 1796
I.8

For Franceschini, as also for his patron, this subject was a welcome pretext for depicting the naked human body: and it is, indeed, with almost Classical smoothness that he renders the group of nymphs attending Diana, who seek modestly to conceal their nakedness from the gaze of a stranger. Franceschini is here indebted to Antiquity, but his true subject is not derived from his interest in its literature. His concern is, rather, the representation of the figure in accordance with the perceived ideal of Antiquity: cool and polished, the generously modelled bodies gleam in the gently transfiguring light. Here, Franceschini has already departed significantly from the style of his teachers, Francesco Albani (1578–1660) and Guido Reni (1575–1642), and has adopted a Neoclassicism that, for this period, is singularly serene: the bodies appear almost artificial, as if removed from real life, and this impression is only dispelled by the incorporation of the episode within a real landscape.

With his response to this commission, Franceschini supplied precisely the sort of painting that the prince loved most: Johann Adam Andreas could, in fact, never have enough of such 'nudes', be it in paintings or in sculptural form. He delighted in every one. And, as demonstrated by his surviving correspondence with Franceschini, this was repeatedly a topic of conversation between the two.

The same archaising ideal of stylised corporeality informs two works by the sculptor Massimiliano Soldani Benzi (1656–1740): the *Dancing Faun* and the *Medici Venus*, wonderfully patinated bronze casts after Classical models. In 1581 the ancient originals faced each other in the Tribuna of the Uffizi in Florence (the model for all subsequent museums of Western art), where they flanked Raphael's *San Giovannino*. Johann Adam Andreas I had seen these figures with his own eyes and was determined to have them for his own gallery – even if only in the form of copies. In his new City Palace in Bankgasse he displayed these

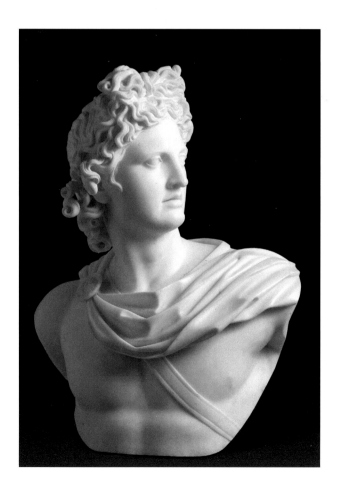

JOHAN ZOFFANY 1733–1810
The Tribuna in the Uffizi, 1772
Oil on canvas, 124 x 155 cm
The Royal Collection, Her Majesty Queen Elizabeth II

ANONYMOUS, ROMAN
Dancing Faun (after the Hellenistic original), 3rd century BC
Marble, height 143 cm
Galleria degli Uffizi, Tribuna, Florence

MASSIMILIANO SOLDANI BENZI 1656–1740
Dancing Faun, *c.* 1705/06
Bronze with reddish brown patina, height 29 cm

copies together in the same room. In his surviving correspondence with Soldani Benzi, the latter congratulates him on his wisdom in deciding to have copies made in bronze, those made in stone never proving able to reproduce the delicate contours of a bronze original, and marble presenting the problem of not being so easily transportable.

The fact that a stone copy of the *Dancing Faun* was made may be attributed to the particular wishes of Johann Adam Andreas I, who wanted to be able to admire this figure not only in Vienna but also at Rossau. Accordingly, he commissioned the sculptor Giovanni Giuliani (1663–1744) in Vienna to make a further copy of the original (the copy was in fact made using the intermediary of a *bozzetto* preserved in the collection of the Heiligenkreuz monastery).

Johann Adam Andreas I von Liechtenstein was one of the first of the eighteenth-century *dilettanti*, whose Grand Tours increasingly took

them to the old cities of Italy and who, with their desire for pictures and sculptures fired by their travels, provided employment for entire generations of artists. A picture of 1772 by Johan Zoffany (1733–1810), now in the Royal Collection in England, records the Florentine Tribuna adorned with numerous works of art that were certainly never there, along with a number of *dilettanti* shown eagerly discussing these pieces. Would we be correct in imagining a similar atmosphere in the Liechtenstein City Palace in Bankgasse, or later in the Garden Palace at Rossau?

In one respect, Soldani Benzi's treatment of Antiquity corresponded entirely with the assumptions of Johann Adam Andreas I von Liechtenstein. And yet the prince was disappointed with the *Bacchus* made by the same artist – this piece being cast not after a model from Antiquity, but after the famous figure by Michelangelo. The original of this

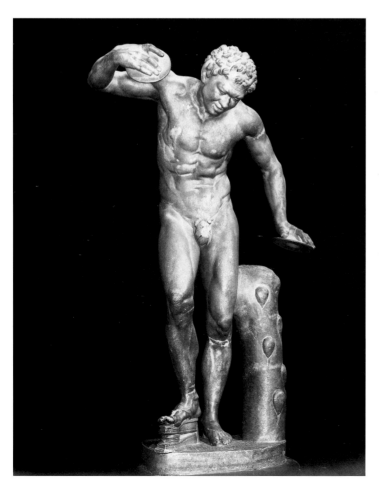

MASSIMILIANO SOLDANI BENZI 1656–1740
Dancing Faun, 1695–97
I.9

GIOVANNI GHISOLFI 1623–83
Roman Ruins with the Three Columns of the Temple of Vespasian
I.10

piece was also to be found in the Uffizi, and it had already been copied in stone by Giambattista Foggini (1652–1737) for the French royal gardens at Marly. For Johann Adam Andreas I, however, it was too far removed from the harmony of Neoclassicism, notwithstanding its rank as an unsurpassable masterpiece from the point of view of technique alone. It is astonishing that, in 1703, at the height of the Baroque period, both he and the artists whose opinions he had sought found Soldani Benzi's copy, upon its arrival in Vienna, to be 'una cosa mal dis-

segnata' (a badly drawn piece), and felt that it had 'un attitudine cativa' (an ugly pose) and an 'idea pesina, e seccha' (was conceptually negative and dry). The prince, who expressed regret that Soldani Benzi had not put his talents to better use, thereby revealed how strong was his commitment to the cool Neoclassicism of Franceschini or to copies made directly from Classical models.
Soldani Benzi's achievement in sculpture at the end of the seventeenth century was to be matched by Giovanni Paolo Pannini (1691–1765) a

GIOVANNI GHISOLFI 1623–83
Roman Ruins
I.11

generation later in his paintings. Pannini supplied a ready market with pictures that testified unequivocally to the grandeur of Antiquity. A native of Piacenza, who had later moved to Rome, he was one of the painters who could draw on his extensive stock of observed, half-invented, and purely fantastical motifs with which to fill canvas after canvas to meet the requirements of a wealthy and educated public. In Rome he had encountered the pictures of Giovanni Ghisolfi (1623–1683), who also painted *capriccios* based on landscapes with

ruins. Pannini was not concerned with the archaeological evidence of the greatness of the past; for him, the architecture of Antiquity was valued for its capacity to evoke a certain mood, as proof of the transience of all earthly creation. Accordingly, he infused his pictures with a certain melancholy, an element of the *memento mori*, and this removed them from the real world into a realm of dreams.

GIOVANNI PAOLO PANNINI 1691–1765
Capriccio with the Most Important Monuments
and Sculptures of Ancient Rome, 1735
I.12

In Pannini's *capriccios*, keenly acquired by Grand Tourists as souvenirs, architecture, sculpture, and the human figure are treated as if equally significant. In his *Capriccio with the Most Important Monuments and Sculptures of Ancient Rome*, Pannini offers an almost unsurpassable survey of such masterpieces. A true panorama of Antiquity unrolls before the spectator: we see *Trajan's Column*, the *Temple of Antoninus and Faustina*, a figure personifying the *River Tiber*, the *Capitoline Lions*, the *Borghese Gladiator*, the *Arch of Constantine*, the *Temple of*

Vesta, the *Pantheon*, the *Pyramid of Cestius*, the *Colosseum*, the *Temple of Castor and Pollux*, the *Basilica of Maxentius*, the *Monument to Marcus Aurelius*, the *Borghese Vase*, the relief of the *Weeping Dacia*, the *Belvedere Torso*, and the porphyry sarcophagus of Empress Costanza. These and numerous others are paraded before us as if all were part of a stage set of the Eternal City.
If the Pantheon in Pannini's *capriccio* is removed to an entirely new location that bears almost no resemblance to reality, and if, in his

GIOVANNI PAOLO PANNINI 1691–1765

The Interior of the Pantheon in Rome, 1735

I.13

Interior of the Pantheon in Rome, the ancient temple to all the gods is encountered in its (new, eighteenth-century) use as a temple to the single God of Christianity, the architecture of Antiquity is nonetheless populated with staffage that is contemporary. We thereby experience this Pantheon as a tangible work of architecture, used by contemporaries of the artist, and perhaps no longer primarily perceived as part of the remains of Antiquity. This *veduta* in particular demonstrates that appropriating the architecture of Antiquity was a matter of course at this time, and how easily a temple dedicated to the worship of a single god could be conjured out of a temple dedicated to the worship of all the gods.

ANDREA LOCATELLI 1695–1741
The Castel Sant'Angelo in Rome
I.15

The French landscape painter Hubert Robert (1733–1808), who in 1766 became a member of the French Academy as a 'peintre des ruines' (painter of ruins), was to become the most celebrated exponent of the genre in the late eighteenth century. With his visionary approach, the painting of ruins entered the next stage of its evolution; and both the emerging science of urbanism and the vogue for landscape gardening owed a great deal to his ideas. It was certainly no coincidence that, in 1778, Robert was appointed 'dessinateur des jardins du Roi' (draughtsman of the king's gardens). From that date on, ruins were generally regarded as one of the most interesting additions that could be made to a garden.

Robert, too, turned his attention to the Pantheon in Rome, and was able to draw attention to an entirely new aspect of this building. Robert's Pantheon, which is raised on a tall base, became an urbanistically defined monument and it occupies a dominating position at the end of a canal. Years later, Pietro Nobile's church of *San Antonio in Trieste* was inspired by this motif, while Antonio Canova's *Tempietto in Possagno* similarly drew on the masterpiece of Antiquity to achieve dominance within its own urban setting. It was as if Antiquity had become a box of building blocks, from which individual elements could be drawn at will.

HUBERT ROBERT 1733–1808

Capriccio with the Pantheon and the Porto di Ripetta, 1761

I.16

HYACINTHE RIGAUD 1659–1743
Portrait of Prince Joseph Wenzel I
von Liechtenstein (1696–1772), 1740
I.17

The head of the House of Liechtenstein by this time was Prince Joseph Wenzel I (1696–1772), an avid collector and an eager patron of the arts. While enchanted by the Rococo throughout most of his life, in his final years his evolving tastes also accommodated the emerging current of Neoclassicism. In Paris the prince had himself painted, twice, by the French portraitist Rigaud who was probably the greatest of the period, in each case ensuring that he was recorded in his full regalia and with an almost imperial demeanour. He must have been a proud man, if we are to judge by the portrait painted by the Neapolitan Francesco Solimena (1657–1747). To mark his appointment as Austrian Ambassador he ordered a luxury vehicle from the best manufacturers in Paris, his celebrated *Golden Carriage*, which was both technologically and stylistically one of the most advanced of its day. It was in this carriage that Joseph Wenzel von Liechtenstein would arrive at Versailles and at the Louvre; and it was also in this carriage that Isabella of Parma, the bride of the later Emperor Josef II, made the journey from Parma to Vienna. At that time Joseph Wenzel was more or less alone in Vienna in his taste for the refined art of French Rococo.

For his residence in Ebergassing, Joseph Wenzel commissioned Gabriel Mollinarolo with two Rococo sculptures, which are among the most important in Austria. It was recently possible to acquire these masterpieces for the Princely Collections, and they now flank the main entrance to the palace, just as they once stood guard on the bridge in front of the residence in Ebergassing. They, too, are informed by a high regard for the art of Antiquity – albeit, in the truest sense of the word, in quite another guise!

BERNARDO BELLOTTO 1720–80
The Liechtenstein Garden Palace in Vienna
Seen from the East, 1759/60
I.19

In their vigorous suggestion of movement they furnish as striking a contrast as is possible with the even polish of a *Venus* by Soldani Benzi. This in turn is a reminder of how unresolved was the question of taste at this period. This was the outcome of the distinct generations and personalities of the collectors, but it was also an instructive reminder of the various sides in the personality of a single collector, such as Joseph Wenzel von Liechtenstein. This patron, so keen to commission exuberant Rococo sculpture, also collected works of early Neoclassicism. The paintings *Hercules at the Crossroads* and *Venus*

Presenting Aeneas Armour Forged by Vulcan by Pompeo Batoni (1708 –87) – second in importance only to Anton Raffael Mengs (1728–79) among painters of this period in Rome – show how Joseph Wenzel was also collecting in accordance with the spirit of the times. Both paintings, acquired and perhaps also commissioned by him, hung in his private picture gallery in the Liechtenstein Palace in Herrengasse in Vienna (it was only towards the end of the eighteenth century that this and the fideicommissum property in Bankgasse
were re-built to form a single structure).

BERNARDO BELLOTTO 1720–80
The Liechtenstein Garden Palace in Vienna
Seen from its Belvedere, 1759/60
I.18

Prince Joseph Wenzel decided to have himself depicted standing proudly in front of his suburban palace, which was later to become the Liechtenstein picture gallery. Today, we still have two of the (probably) original three views that he commissioned from Bernardo Bellotto (1721–80). These, while epitomising the spirit of Roman *grandezza* in Vienna, are recorded in a manner that is topographically accurate. In both pictures the patron is shown contemplating a detailed rendering of his palace and extensive gardens. The documentary value of these pictures is considerable, not only with regard to the appearance and colour of the palace and its relation to the Belvedere as of 1760, but also in recording, for the last time, the extensive Baroque garden with its statuary. Starting in 1773, the sculptures and vases were auctioned off and work was begun on an English-style landscape garden. In 1787 Joseph Hardtmuth appeared on the scene (he was to be appointed architect to the prince in 1790) and, both at the suburban palace and at numerous other locations, was responsible for an upheaval that would introduce Neoclassicism, in the strict sense of that term, to the House of Liechtenstein.

I.1 / p. 44
Hermanus Posthumus (c. 1513/14–88)
Landscape with Roman Ruins, 1536
Oil on canvas, 96 x 141 cm
Signed and dated on the fragment of the foot to
right of centre: Herman posthum pingeb 1.5.3.6.
Inv. no. GE 740
Provenance: acquired in 1983 from a private col-
lection by Prince Franz Josef II von und zu Liecht-
enstein

I.2 / p. 48
Maerten van Heemskerck (1498–1574)
Landscape with St Jerome, 1547
Oil on canvas, 105 x 161 cm
Signed and dated at lower left: Martinus
Heemskerck fecit 1547
Provenance: first recorded as part of the Schön-
born-Buchheim Collection, Vienna in 1746

I.3 / p. 46
Benvenuto Tisi, called Il Garofalo (1481–1559)
The Apotheosis of Hercules, c. 1539
Oil on canvas, 86 x 116 cm
Inv. no. GE 2136
Provenance: until 1823 in a Viennese private
collection; thereafter in a northern European
princely collection; acquired in 2004 by
Prince Hans-Adam II von und zu Liechtenstein

I.4 / p. 50
Anonymous, Bolognese
Bust of Flora, c. 1700
Marble, height 68 cm
Inv. no. SK 1369

I.5 / p. 50
Anonymous, French
Bust of the Dying Alexander (after the Antique
original), 2nd half of 17th century
Marble, height 79 cm
Inv. no. SK 12
Provenance: acquired in 1999 by Prince Hans-
Adam II von und zu Liechtenstein at auction at
Sotheby's, London

I.6 / p. 51
Marcantonio Franceschini (1648–1729)
Diana and Actaeon, 1692/98
Oil on canvas, 481 x 254 cm
Inv. no. GE 69
Provenance: commissioned in 1698 by Prince
Johann Adam Andreas I von und zu Liechtenstein
as part of the decoration of the Liechtenstein
Garden Palace at Rossau

I.7 / p. 52
Anonymous
Bust of Apollo (after the *Apollo Belvedere*),
18th century
Marble, height 70 cm
Inv. no. SK 7
Provenance: recorded in the library of the City
Palace in Bankgasse, Vienna, in 1848

I.8 / p. 52
Giovanni Pisani (1757–1839)
Bust of Zeus (after the Antique original), 1796
Marble, height 49 cm
Signed and dated: GIUSEPPE PISANI ROMA 1796
Private collection, Vienna

I.9 / p. 55
Massimiliano Soldani Benzi (1656–1740)
Dancing Faun, 1695–97
Bronze with reddish brown patina, height 139 cm
Inv. no. SK 541, companion piece to inv. nos.
SK 537 and SK 573
Provenance: commissioned in 1695, along with the
Medici Venus (SK 537), by Prince Johann Adam
Andreas I von Liechtenstein; both works acquired
in 1702

I.10 / p. 56
Giovanni Ghisolfi (1623–83)
*Roman Ruins with the Three Columns
of the Temple of Vespasian*
Oil on canvas, 49 x 66 cm
Inv. no. GE 214
Provenance: first recorded as part of the
Princely Collections in 1805

I.11 / p. 56
Giovanni Ghisolfi (1623–83)
Roman Ruins
Oil on canvas, 49 x 66 cm
Inv. no. GE 219
Provenance: first recorded as part of the
Princely Collections in 1805

I.12 / p. 58
Giovanni Paolo Pannini (1691–1765)
*Capriccio with the Most Important Monuments
and Sculptures of Ancient Rome*, 1735
Oil on canvas, 126 x 180 cm
Inv. no. GE 2132
Provenance: in a private collection in England;
sold in 1976 to a French private collection at
auction at Sotheby's, London; acquired in 2003
by Prince Hans-Adam II von und zu Liechtenstein

I.13 / pp. 59–60
Giovanni Paolo Pannini (1691–1765)
The Interior of the Pantheon in Rome, 1735
Oil on canvas, 127 x 99 cm
Signed and dated on the pedestal of the column to
the left: JO. PAULUS PANINI MDCCXXXV
Inv. no. GE 166
Provenance: until 1791 probably owned by George
Gordon, Lord Haddo; until 1969 in the possession
of Major David Gordon, Earl of Haddo, Aberdeen-
shire; sold at auction at Sotheby's, London, in
1969; acquired in 2001 by Prince Hans-Adam II
von und zu Liechtenstein

I.14 / p. 61
(?) Rieger
View of the Colosseum in Rome, 1609
Drawing in pen and ink with grey and brown wash
over charcoal on paper, 31 x 41cm
Inscription at lower right: il Colloseo di Roma
1609. Rieger la meza Parte
Inscription on the verso: Parte de Colloseo /
1609.R.
Inv. no. GR 1878
Provenance: acquired in 1983 by Prince Franz
Joseph II von und zu Liechtenstein

I.15 / p. 62
Andrea Locatelli (1695–1741)
The Castel Sant'Angelo in Rome
Oil on canvas, 155 x 235 cm
Inv. no. GE 220
Provenance: probably acquired by Prince Johann
Adam Andreas I von Liechtenstein (first recorded
as part of the Princely Collections in 1780)

I.16 / p. 63
Hubert Robert (1733–1808)
*Capriccio with the Pantheon and the Porto
di Ripetta*, 1761
Oil on canvas, 102 x 146 cm
Signed and dated on a plaque above the niche
of the fountain: ...D..CHOISEVL / H.ROBERTI.../
..ACADEMIAE.. / QVADR...1761
Inv. no. GE 511
Provenance: acquired in 1951 by Prince Franz
Josef II von und zu Liechtenstein from the holdings
of the Hessisches Landesmusuem, Darmstadt

I.17 / pp. 64–65
Hyacinthe Rigaud (1659–1743)
*Portrait of Prince Joseph Wenzel I von Liechten-
stein (1696–1772)*, 1740
Oil on canvas, 146 x 114 cm
Signed and dated on the verso: Peint à Paris
par Hyacinthe Rigaud, Chevalier de L'ordre de
S. Michel, en 1740.
Inv. no. GE 1496
Provenance: commissioned in 1740 by Prince
Joseph Wenzel von Liechtenstein

I.18 / p. 67
Bernardo Bellotto (1720–80)
*The Liechtenstein Garden Palace in Vienna Seen
from its Belvedere*, 1759/60
Oil on canvas, 100 x 159 cm
Inv. no. GE 889, companion piece to inv. no.
GE 887
Provenance: commissioned in 1760, along with
*The Liechtenstein Garden Palace in Vienna Seen
from the East* (inv. no. GE 887), by Prince Joseph
Wenzel von Liechtenstein

I.19 / p. 66
Bernardo Bellotto (1720–80)
*The Liechtenstein Garden Palace in Vienna Seen
from the East*, 1759/60
Oil on canvas, 100 x 160 cm
Inv. no. GE 887, companion piece to inv. no.
GE 889
Provenance: commissioned in 1760, along with
*The Liechtenstein Garden Palace in Vienna Seen
from its Belvedere* (inv. no. GE 889), by Prince
Joseph Wenzel I von Liechtenstein

I.20 / not illus.
Anonymous, Viennese
Console table, 19th century
Gilt limewood and pine, height 81 cm,
width 133 cm, depth 70 cm
Inv. no. MO 922
Provenance: recorded around 1900 in the
Liechtenstein City Palace in Bankgasse,
Vienna

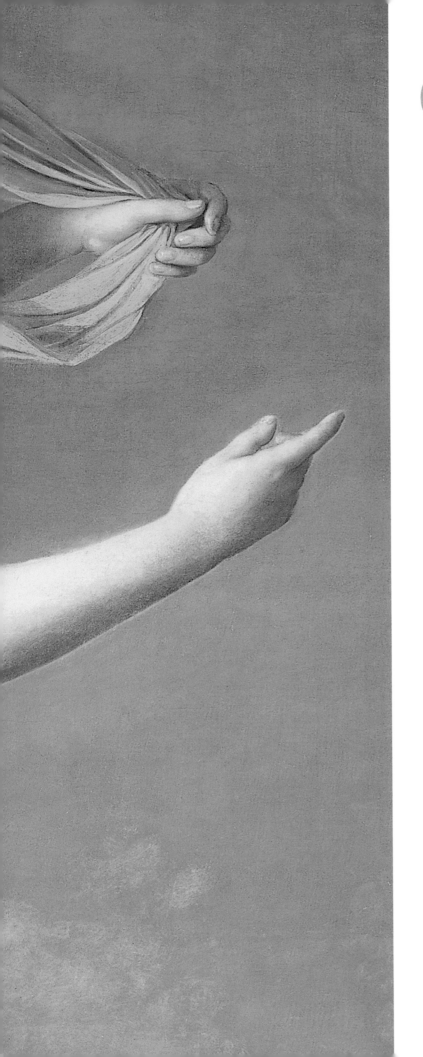

GALLERY II

POLITICS AND ART AT THE TURN OF THE EIGHTEENTH TO THE NINETEENTH CENTURY

The *Seated Statue of Princess Leopoldine von Esterházy* by the Italian sculptor Antonio Canova (1757–1822) is a dominant presence. She appears to take charge of the proceedings at the centre of this room, which is a good place to gain an overview of the entire network of interrelationships that links the other sculptures and paintings found here.

In the summer of 1805, when Canova came to Vienna in connection with the installation of his *Tomb of Marie Christine of Austria* in the Augustinerkirche, despite the chaos and uncertainty of this period of Napoleonic Wars he was prompted to extend to several months what was evidently a most enjoyable sojourn. Since 1786 his Viennese followers had been able to admire his *Minotaur Group* at the Fries Palace, and in 1798 they had the chance to meet him in person during his

first stay in Vienna, to their delight finding him to be not only a sculptor of genius but also a congenial man.

It was during Canova's second stay in Vienna that he was commissioned to make the *Seated Statue of Princess Leopoldine von Esterházy*. He was approached by Leopoldine's father, Prince Nikolaus II Esterházy, whose request was benevolently seconded and supported by her fiancé, Moritz von Liechtenstein. In 1806 a mask was taken of Leopoldine's face, and a little later Moritz von Liechtenstein informed Canova that a bust in wax had also been made, but that its outlines would need to be rendered more firmly if it were to serve as the model for a work in marble. The case containing the wax bust then made its way from Vienna, via Trieste, to Rome. We are very well informed on all these developments thanks to the enthusiastic correspondence of this period

LEOPOLDINA ESTERHÁZY
M·DCCC·V

ANTONIO CANOVA 1757–1822

Seated Statue of Princess Leopoldine von Esterházy,
later von Liechtenstein (1788–1846), 1805–15
II.1

ALBERT CHRISTOPH DIES 1775–1822

View of the Landscape Garden of the Esterházy Palace at
Eisenstadt with the Temple of Leopoldine and the Gloriette
by Charles de Moreau in the Background, 1807
Esterházy-Privatstiftung, Eisenstadt

FRANZ ANTON ZAUNER 1746–1822
Seated Figure of Clio, 1779
II.2

between Canova and Count Lamberg. By this means we learn that, in 1807, Nikolaus II Esterházy was sent into raptures by Canova's first sketches, but became disgruntled on realising how slowly the work was progressing. His discontent turned to astonishment when he grasped that the sculpture in hand was not in fact the Venus he had envisaged (for which he had planned a temple in the park of Esterházy palace): Canova's notion of a muse shown drawing seemed to him far too profane for the hallowed setting he had envisioned for it. In order to arrive at a clearer idea of Canova's scheme, Esterházy asked him, through Lamberg, for an outline drawing, also enquiring at this point as to the sum that the artist would charge for the finished marble figure (apparently, there had as yet been no discussion of this aspect of the commission).

Over the next few years Canova's output was much influenced by the impact on taste in Europe of Napoleon Bonaparte (1769–1821). In Paris the artist produced a number of works for Napoleon, and he also planned the *Seated Concordia* for the French Empress Marie Louise; in discussing this with her he mentioned his earlier figure of Leopoldine, which was then underway. In 1810 Nikolaus II Esterházy himself sent to Paris to attend the wedding of Marie Louise (1791–1847), and in 1814 he acquired the Viennese Kaunitz Palace, where he installed his picture gallery. He resolved, however, to abandon his ambitious scheme for a new palace at Eisenstadt.

On 19 May 1815 Canova wrote to inform his patron in Vienna that his work on the figure of Leopoldine was finished and to state what was in fact a relatively low sale price (on account of the imperfections in the block of marble used for this piece). In mid-1818 the figure arrived in Vienna in good condition, but Nikolaus II Esterházy demanded that Canova supply an additional work free of charge in compensation for the blemishes in the stone. In 1820, accordingly, Canova completed work on a base for his *Seated Statue of Princess Leopoldine von Esterházy*. In 1822 the statue was moved from Vienna (where it had been provisionally stored in the glasshouse of the palace in the Mariahilf district) to Eisenstadt. Here, it was definitively installed in the *Temple of Leopoldine* in the park of Esterházy palace.

Canova's overall ambition as a sculptor was to devise a means of reconciling the contemporary demands of portraiture with an ideal type derived from the sculpture of Antiquity. The chief Austrian exponent of Neoclassicism in sculpture, Franz Anton Zauner (1746–1822), had begun to adopt a comparable approach to Antiquity as a model while studying in Rome. In 1779 he made for the Academy of Fine Arts in

Vienna a small figure of the Muse Clio – today in the Princely Collections – which overtly quotes models from the time of Emperor Hadrian that were by this date in the Vatican Collections. Zauner had in fact effectively devised a new figure through combining aspects of several in a sequence depicting the Nine Muses: the seated position of Clio and the head of Terpsichore.

In his sculpture of Leopoldine Esterházy, to whom he was said to have felt drawn, Canova also enjoyed setting himself the task of combining an idealised model derived from Antiquity with the spirited princess's true appearance, which he recorded in numerous studies. A bust by Canova now in the Princely Collections occupies a position that is somewhere between the two: it remains uncertain as to whether it would be more correctly titled *Portrait of Princess Leopoldine von Esterházy* or *Bust of Venus Italica*. Canova would come closest to the actual appearance of his sitters not only in his drawings but also in his clay *bozzetti* and, finally, in his full-scale plaster *modelli*. In the case of his sculpture of Princess Leopoldine, examples of all three stages in the working process have been preserved. Unlike his fellow sculptor the Dane Bertel Thorvaldsen (1770–1844), Canova made much of this process of sculptural evolution. He tended to view the outcome of each stage as an autonomous artistic achievement, collecting and preserving these as a precious form of documentation. Thorvaldsen, by contrast, preserved for posterity a far smaller proportion of such intermediate products of sculptural creation.

ANTONIO CANOVA 1757–1822
Bust of Venus Italica or Portrait of Princess Leopoldine
von Esterházy, later von Liechtenstein, *c.* 1805–15
II.4

Both sculptors are themselves present in this room: Canova in a portrait painted by Giovanni Battista Lampi (1751–1830), and Thorvaldsen recorded in old age by the Austrian portrait painter Friedrich von Amerling (1803–87). The first of these was made in 1806, that is to say in precisely those years when Canova was at work on his seated figure of Princess Leopoldine; and in its background we see a detail of the major work that Canova had just installed in Vienna, his *Tomb of Marie Christine of Austria*: the lamenting winged genius resting on the back of a lion. This portrait presents the celebrated artist in his studio as a prince in the realm of art, and the subject appears removed from contemporary everyday life through the Neoclassical aspect of the sumptuous drapery. Like a military commander resting on his baton, he supports himself on the handle of his chisel while the modelling block serves as a support for the laurel wreath.

The portrait of Thorvaldsen was painted in 1843, almost a generation later. It is a striking record of the celebrated Dane as an old man (he was in fact to die the following year). Amerling painted this portrait during his second stay in Rome and must have finished it around autumn of 1842. Thorvaldsen, who left Rome on 1 October of that year, appears to have added his own signature to the picture before the paint had dried.

In Amerling's portrait, too, we encounter an impressive personality, albeit not one conveyed through expansive gesture. Rather, we have the sense of an individual turned in upon himself, who has found inner peace at the end of a lifetime's labours. The subject is depicted so as to eschew any outward expression, in a manner that might be described as 'private' (with all the connotations this term had for the Biedermeier Era) and without any celebration of his profession. Distracting details have been dispensed with, and one can sense the relationship established between the painter and his sitter. More than any of the other numerous portraits of Thorvaldsen, this picture from the Princely Collections confronts the spectator with the subject's character: melancholy appears to be the dominant emotion, and this had indeed found its reflection in the often extreme reserve, even lifelessness, of his sculptures.

GIOVANNI BATTISTA LAMPI 1751–1830

Portrait of the Sculptor Antonio Canova (1757–1822), 1806

II.5

Detail
II.5

ANTONIO CANOVA 1757–1822
Bust of Napoleon Francis, King of Rome (1811–32), 1812
II.7

Napoleon Bonaparte was one of the most influential men of this era. An entire generation was fascinated by his every move. He left a bloody trail across Europe, but at the same time he provided an extraordinary new impetus for cultural life, counting the most important artists of the age among his followers. There were great commissions in jubilant abundance, with the result that Canova, too, followed Napoleon to Paris. The Princely Collections possess one of the many portrait busts of Napoleon to issue from Canova's studio. In this piece the artist presents Napoleon *all'antica*. A bust also exists of Napoleon's son, born to him in Paris on 20 March 1811 from his union with the Austrian Princess Marie Louise. No birth was celebrated with greater pomp than that of this longed-for heir. The 'Emperor of the French' gave his son, at birth, the title of 'King of Rome'. In 1814, after Napoleon had been banished to the island of St Helena, Marie Louise returned to Vienna with her son. There, under the protection of his grandfather, Austrian Emperor Franz I, Napoleon Francis was brought up at the Viennese imperial court. Suffering from consumption, however, this 'Duke of Reichstadt' (the title he had been granted in Vienna) died at the young age of twenty-one.

Canova's portrait bust, signed and dated 1812, shows the 'king' at the age of one, as a somewhat thickset child. It was, however, not made from life but based on sketches that had been sent to Canova in Rome.

STUDIO OF ANTONIO CANOVA 1757–1822
Bust of Napoleon I, Emperor of France (1769–1821),
early 19th century
II.8

PIETRO TENERANI 1798–1869
Bust of a Girl, 1837
II.10

ANONYMOUS, AUSTRIAN
Bust of Pallas Athena, late 18th century
II.9

How light and carefree, by contrast, is the *Bust of a Girl* by Pietro Tenerani (1798–1869), which seems so real that it almost breathes. This work of 1837 is by a follower of Canova in Rome, who accomplished within his own oeuvre the transition from Neoclassicism to Historicism, and it evinces a new, and substantially less academic, approach.

There is no doubt that the House of Liechtenstein played its own part in the eclipse of Napoleon. Prince Johann I (1760–1836), in his capacity as a military leader, met Napoleon on many occasions and was substantially involved in his first significant military defeat at the Battle of Aspern on 21 and 22 May 1809. The prince is to be found in this room in a portrait painted by Giovanni Battista Lampi.

JOHANN PETER KRAFFT 1780–1856
Archduke Karl (1771–1847) with his Staff
at the Battle of Aspern, 1820
II.11

In 1813 Johann Peter Krafft (1780–1856) was commissioned by the legislature of the Crownland of Lower Austria to depict the battle for the Hall of Honour of the Invalidenhaus, the result being his extensive mural showing *Archduke Karl with his Staff at the Battle of Aspern*, completed in 1819. In 1820 Krafft painted a second, smaller version for Prince Johann I von Liechtenstein. In Krafft's composition we see the military leaders with Archduke Karl (1771–1847) at their head, followed by Prince Liechtenstein. Krafft lay great store by the detail in his portrayal of each commander, shown in a white uniform decorated with all his orders. Nor, however, did Krafft hesitate to convey some-

thing of the wretchedness of the battle, showing the wounded and dying in the middle distance so as to constitute a secondary compositional focus at the left of the canvas.

In 1816, over a year after the post-Napoleonic re-ordering of Europe achieved at the Congress of Vienna, Lampi painted a portrait of Prince Johann I von Liechtenstein. He, too, appears in the white uniform of a general, in this case with the Orders of the Great Cross and Star and of the Golden Fleece, with which he had been decorated in 1806. This portrait, too, painted when the prince was fifty-six and symbolically including a canon in its background, clearly depicts him as a military

GIOVANNI BATTISTA LAMPI 1751–1830
Portrait of Prince Johann I von Liechtenstein (1760–1836),
1816
II.12

PETER EDUARD STRÖHLING 1768–after 1826
Portrait of Prince Alois I von Liechtenstein (1759–1805),
1794
II.13

man. The fact that he also achieved much in other fields can be touched on only briefly here. Like his brother Alois I von Liechtenstein (1759–1805), recorded in a portrait of 1794 by the German artist Peter Eduard Ströhling (1768–after 1826), Prince Johann was an extremely enthusiastic builder. It was he who appointed Joseph Hardtmuth as his architect. In this function Hardtmuth designed the new residences in Littau, at Adamsthal near Brno, and at Hadersfeld near Klosterneuburg. In and around Vienna Hardtmuth was responsible for the Hussars' Temple and the pleasure palace on the Schüttel in the

Prater district, though Joseph Kornhäusel eventually assumed responsibility for this last. At Eisgrub Hardtmuth oversaw the transformation of the Baroque garden into one in the English style. Here, he also built the Hansenburg, the new manor house, the Temple of Diana, the palace on the lake, the colonnade at the top of Raistenberg, and the hunting lodge at Pohansko.

This rage for building – in the case of a Liechtenstein it was almost a case of taking owls to Athens – also moved Prince Alois I to have the old palace in Herrengasse thoroughly reconstructed. Not least among

FRIEDRICH OELENHAINZ 1745–1804
Portrait of the Future Prince Johann I
von Liechtenstein (1760–1836), 1776
II.14

FRIEDRICH OELENHAINZ 1745–1804
Portrait of the Future Prince Alois I
von Liechtenstein (1759–1805), 1776
II.15

the reasons for this undertaking was the resolve to link the library with the new rooms and to extend the collection of prints and drawings. In all probability, one of the prince's most significant contributions with regard to the world of art was his decision of 1807 to transfer the picture gallery from the City Palace in Bankgasse to the Garden Palace at Rossau, for the gallery in its new location was also accessible to the public. Sadly, however, hardly anything has survived of the palace in Herrengasse – a masterpiece of Neoclassical architecture in Austria – except for the library, which in the early twentieth century was itself moved to the Garden Palace. The little that has been preserved is a testament to the extremely high quality of the decoration of this building. This includes several candelabra and two frames for pictures by the French portrait painter Elisabeth Vigée-Lebrun (1755–1842). All of these share the same graceful and extremely finely detailed carving. This great French portrait painter stopped in Vienna during the extensive travels she undertook in 1793–94. Here, in the capital of the Habsburg Monarchy and home to its rulers, she was immediately inundated with portrait commissions. For the Liechtenstein family she painted two very large portraits for the palace in Herrengasse, which was at that very moment being rebuilt in the latest architectural style and decorated accordingly. With her portrait of Karoline von Liechten-

stein (1768–1831), the wife of Prince Alois I, and of his sisters Maria Josepha Hermenegilde Esterházy (1768–1845), married since 1783 to Prince Nikolaus II Esterházy, Vigée-Lebrun delivered two masterly testaments to the outstanding abilities that by this date had already assured her of broad international recognition.

Vigée-Lebrun informs both portraits with mythological content, showing Karoline von Liechtenstein as the goddess Iris, and Maria Josepha Hermenegilde Esterházy as Ariadne on Naxos. It is possible, moreover, that the *Portrait of Princess Leopoldine Adelgunde von Liechtenstein* by Friedrich Oelenhainz (1745–1804), who in 1776 also recorded this sitter's siblings Maria Jospeha Hemenegilde Esterházy, Alois and Johann, was intended to allude to the strong connection, in the late eighteenth century, of the House of Liechtenstein with music.

This embraced the extraordinary role adopted by Maria Josepha Hermenegilde Esterházy, for whose name day Joseph Haydn had composed six great Masses before 1802. The last of these, the Harmony Mass, was performed on 8 September 1802, under the direction of the seventy-year-old composer, in the Bergkirche at Eisenstadt. Prince Ludwig Starhemberg recorded in his diary the splendour with which this occasion was celebrated: To begin with, all the guests paid their respects to the princess; then everyone went in a large procession of

FRIEDRICH OELENHAINZ 1745–1804
Portrait of Princess Leopoldine Adelgunde
von Liechtenstein (1754–1823), 1776
II.16

FRIEDRICH OELENHAINZ 1745–1804
Portrait of Princess Maria Josepha Hermenegilde
von Liechtenstein (1768–1845), 1776
II.17

ELISABETH VIGÉE-LEBRUN 1755–1842
Portrait of Princess Karoline von Liechtenstein, née Countess
von Manderscheit (1768–1831), as Iris, 1793
II.18

ELISABETH VIGÉE-LEBRUN 1755–1842
Portrait of Princess Maria Josepha Hermenegilde
von Liechtenstein, later Princess Esterházy (1768–1845),
as Ariadne on Naxos, 1793
II.19

GIOVANNI BATTISTA LAMPI 1755–1830
Portrait Sketch of Princess Josepha Sophie von Liechtenstein,
née Countess zu Fürstenberg-Weitra (1776–1848)
II.20

many carriages to Mass in the Bergkirche at Eisenstadt. After the service there was a banquet at the palace 'as excellent as it was generous, and accompanied by music. The prince drank to the health of the princess and in answer there came fanfares and gun salutes – and so it went on, they drank to me, too, and to Haydn, who was dining with us and to whom I raised my glass. Having eaten, we donned evening dress and went to a ball, which was really superb, like a ball at Court; the princess opened the dancing with her daughter in a minuet. After that we only danced waltzes …'. It was to mark the same occasion,

the princess's name day, that Beethoven was commissioned to provide his Mass in C Major, first performed at Eisenstadt in 1807.
Informed by quite other expectations than were the portraits of Vigée-Lebrun (which were as if tailored to suit their presentation in the then exceptionally modern interior of the palace in Herrengasse) or the paintings by Oelenhainz (which were firmly integrated into the decoration of the palace at Eisgrub, in the so-called 'family room') is the small portrait drawing of Josepha Sophie von Liechtenstein, née Fürstenberg, since 1792 the wife of Johann I von Liechtenstein. This sketch is

ANGELICA KAUFFMANN 1741–1807
Modello for the Portrait of Ferdinand IV, King of Naples
and both Sicily (1759–1825) and his Family, 1782/83
II.22

a marvellous example of how close a relationship had been established between the painter and his sitter and how directly he was able to reflect this experience in his work. With loose, rapid brushstrokes, he has superbly captured the character of his subject. There is no suggestion at all here of an 'official' record.

This portrait has traditionally been ascribed to the German artist Heinrich von Füger (1751–1818), who achieved a similar directness in his relationship with the sitters of whom he produced portrait miniatures. There is, however, a possibility that this lively sketch was the work of

Giovanni Battista Lampi, who had in fact recorded the sitter's husband, Prince Johann I von Liechtenstein, in a comparably immediate fashion, albeit in a quite different type of work. The *Double Portrait of Countesses Caroline and Zoe Tomatis*, now in the collection of the Österreichische Galerie Belvedere, is distinguished by its similarly lively rendering and its vigorous brushwork and was likewise long thought to be the work of Füger.

Detail
II.22

ANGELICA KAUFFMANN 1741–1807
Sketch for the Portrait of Ferdinand IV, King of Naples
and both Sicily (1759–1825) and his Family, 1782
II.21

Equally striking on account of its liveliness is the *bozzetto* by the
Swiss painter Angelica Kauffmann (1741–1807) for her *Portrait of Ferdinand IV, King of Naples and both Sicily (1759–1825) and his Family*.
The extraordinarily large finished painting, over four metres wide,
hangs in Naples. The life-size figures we find here are those of the
king, his consort, Queen Marie Karoline, a daughter of Maria Theresia,
and six of her children. The royal family is posed against the background of a park landscape and is dressed accordingly. The bucolic
ideal of a rural life and the ideas of the French philosopher Jean
Jacques Rousseau both inform this composition, which reflects the
corresponding shift of taste among patrons. These no longer desired
to have themselves recorded – one is tempted to say 'photographed' –
for posterity in the context of their palaces and other imposing residences. They wished to be shown, rather, under God's open sky.
The evolution of this painting had been precisely recorded. On 7 April
1782 Kauffmann left Venice after a brief stay there; she then remained

in Naples until the start of November. During September and October
she painted a number of individual portraits of the royal family in
preparation for her work on the large picture, which she executed in
Rome in 1783. The next year the painting was transported to Naples,
and since 1893 it has hung in the Museo di Capodimonte. To begin
with, Kauffmann produced a rapidly annotated sketch, almost reminis-
cent of the work of the English painter Thomas Gainsborough
(1727–88). The *modello*, a later version of the painting most closely
resembling the finished composition, in fact includes the 'ghost' of
a seventh child (this was the short-lived Prince Joseph, who died in
1783); although painted out, he nonetheless remains visible. By comparison with the finished composition, the sketch and the *modello*,
both in the Princely Collections, are distinguished by their directness
and liveliness, and it is through these qualities that they provide such
a vivid image of the royal family.

ed French interior. On 10 August 1792 the princess was imprisoned along with the Queen in the temple. She refused to swear an oath against the monarchy and on 3 September she was executed. Her severed head was then placed on a pike and paraded in front of the window of the Queen's prison cell.

The portrait painted by Hickel in Paris in 1788 gives no hint of the dark events that were to follow and shows the princess dressed in a white satin gown and seated at her desk in an everyday setting that seems almost entirely uncontrived. There is great brilliance in the rendering of diverse fabrics: the gleaming satin of the dress, the carpet with its floral pattern, and the wood of the desk. This in particular gives us a very immediate sense of the refinement and opulence of cultivated living in France on the eve of the French Revolution, of all that within a few years was to be swallowed up by a wave of brutal aggression.

In 1817 Heinrich von Füger painted his *Prometheus Brings Fire to Mankind*, uniting in a single work of art the ideals of painting and of sculpture. According to mythology, Prometheus, son of a Titan, stole fire from the gods in order, against their will, to give life to a creature that he had made. In Füger's picture Prometheus occupies almost the entire picture plane, his body modelled in warm, glowing colour; at his feet there lies a lifeless human body, formed out of clay and gleaming with a sallow grey-green. It still lacks the warmth of the divine fire that will bestow life and the corresponding colour. The excitement of this picture derives from the contrast to be found within its chromatic range, but also from the refined distinction in the modelling of both skin and clay: we eagerly await the transfer of the spark of life to the limp body. Füger's picture is impressive on account of its large scale: the muscular body of Prometheus resembles a colossal statue from Antiquity, recalling the horse tamers on Monte Cavallo in Rome, which during the Renaissance were thought to be the work of Phidias and Praxiteles.

In Prometheus Füger took on a mythological figure that, since the Renaissance, had been associated with the artist as creator. For Füger, however, Prometheus was also a torch-bearer for the rejection of the Baroque: in almost no other work of his is the language of Neoclassicism more sharply formulated than in this painting. A *bozzetto* for this composition has also been preserved, and this has a pendant, dated 1817, *Hercules Freeing Prometheus*. We can, therefore, date the picture now in the Princely Collections to the last years of Füger's life.

A contemporary of Kauffmann, and a painter who led almost as restless a life, was Anton Hickel (1745–98). Like Kauffmann, he spent much time in England, where he produced a sensational painting of a debate in the Houses of Parliament, featuring ninety-six life-size portraits. Earlier in his career he had been based in Paris, where he was able to win the trust of Marie Antoinette and her chief lady-in-waiting, Princesse de Lamballe, shown here by Hickel in an elegantly decorat-

< HEINRICH VON FÜGER 1751–1818
Prometheus Brings Fire to Mankind, 1817
II.24

FRANZ ANTON ZAUNER 1746–1822
Nymph with a Putto, Figures for a Fountain, after 1797
II.25

The Austrian sculptor Franz Anton Zauner (1746–1822) was able, with his reclining nymph, actually formed out of clay, both to create just such a work of art and then to bring it to life by means of metal melted in fire. The figure was assuredly intended for a fountain, but we have no certain knowledge concerning its provenance. In the early 1920s it stood packed in a crate in front of the library of the Garden Palace at Rossau, and in 1933 the figure was made part of a fountain in the pond at the park at Rossau. As Hermann Burg mentions in his monograph on Zauner, we are not able to say with any certainty whether it is linked with that 'over-life-size group of a nymph and two children in the former palace of Count Fries in Neulengbach near Vienna'. Neulengbach was acquired by the Fries family in 1797, suggesting that the figure was made shortly after this. The Liechtenstein family acquired the palace in 1823 but sold it again in 1920, which could well explain the appearance of the figure in a crate at the Garden Palace in the early 1920s.

The nymph falls entirely within the tradition of Viennese lead-tin figures made very much under the spell of Georg Raphael Donner (1693–1741), to whom this work was long ascribed. The Moll family of sculptors used a lead-tin alloy as their preferred material, as was also the

JOHANN MARTIN FISCHER 1740–1820
The Dream of St Joseph (second version of a relief
for the Josef Fountain in the Graben, Vienna),
c. 1804
II.26

form to the clay and thus breathes life into it, is nowhere more palpable than here.

Much the same can be said of a relief of *c.* 1804 by Johann Martin Fischer (1740–1820), *The Dream of St Joseph*. This is the remarkably well-preserved second version of the relief intended for the principal face of the pedestal of the *Josef Fountain* in the Graben in Vienna. In 1803 the Mayor of Vienna resolved to replace the fountains of Saints Joseph and Leopold in the Graben, both being in a poor state of repair, and Fischer was commissioned to design and execute both replacements.

As in the work of Zauner, that of Fischer still evinces traces of the local stylistic heritage: an orientation to the achievement of Donner, whose *Providence Fountain* Fischer had restored in 1801 and with whose overall sculptural output he was very familiar. However, although Zauner and Fischer were contemporaries, they progressed in very different directions. The eventually radical Neoclassicism of Zauner, who had trained in Italy, was the opposite of Fischer's manner, itself a very personal style that was in part still rooted in the late Baroque.

case with Franz Xaver Messerschmidt (1736–83), who is represented in the present exhibition by an elegant portrait head from a private collection in Vienna. Zauner creates a group that is formally pleasing from many different angles through his deft combination of the nymph (whose left hand holds a jug, out of which water bubbles into the basin) with the putto (who holds a fish from whose mouth water also spouts). Like all lead-tin figures, those made by Zauner derive their charm from the visual appeal of the surface of the material, for none other is better at conveying the impression of the wet clay from which the initial model was made. The 'Promethean' hand of the sculptor, which lends

ASCRIBED TO FRANZ XAVER MESSERSCHMIDT 1736–83

Bust of a Man, *c.* 1770

II.27

JOSEPH HARDTMUTH 1758–1816, design
Two panels for the decoration of the Liechtenstein palace
in Herrengasse, Vienna, *c.* 1792
II.28

JOSEHPH HARDTMUTH 1758–1816, design
Candelabrum with girandole (from an original series of eight, probably made for the decoration of the Liechtenstein palace in Herrengasse, Vienna), *c.* 1790
II.29

ANONYMOUS, GENOESE
Console table, late 18th century
II.30

II.1 / pp. 72–74
Antonio Canova (1757–1822)
Seated Statue of Princess Leopoldine von Ester-
házy, later von Liechtenstein (1788–1846),
1805–15
Marble, height 146 cm, width 110 cm, depth
150 cm
Esterházy-Privatstiftung, Eisenstadt
Provenance: commissioned by Prince Nikolaus II
von Esterházy, father of the subject, at the suggestion of her fiancé, Prince Moritz von Liechtenstein,
for the *Temple of Leopoldine* in the park of Esterházy Palace at Eisenstadt

II.2 / p. 76
Franz Anton Zauner (1746–1822)
Seated Figure of Clio, 1779
Marble, height 80 cm
Signed and dated on chair: F. ZAUNER . FECIT
ROMAE / ANNO 1779.
Inscription on the cartouche: MARIAE THERESIAE /
IMPER . HUNGAR . ET BOHEM . / REGINAE . AUG .
P.F. APOSTOL . RERUM GESTARUM MEMORIA
Inv. no. SK 617
Provenance: made in 1779 for the Viennese
Academy of Fine Arts; from 1780 in the Viennese
collection of its patron, Prince Wenzel Anton von
Kaunitz

II.3 / p. 77
Marten Jozef Geeraerts (1707–91)
Children and Amoretti, 1752
Oil on canvas, 77 x 124 cm
Signed and dated at lower right: M.J.Geeraerts /
F. Antverpiae.1752
Inv. no. GE 530
Provenance: acquired by Prince Joseph Wenzel
von Liechtenstein

II.4 / p. 78
Antonio Canova (1757–1822)
Bust of Venus Italica or *Portrait of Princess*
Leopoldine von Esterházy, later von Liechtenstein,
c. 1805–15
Marble, height 62 cm
Inv. no. SK 1406
Provenance: acquired in 1964 by Prince Franz
Josef II von und zu Liechtenstein from Count
Alois Podstatzky

II.5 / pp. 79–80
Giovanni Battista Lampi (1751–1830)
Portrait of the Sculptor Antonio Canova
(1757–1822), 1806
Oil on canvas, 113 x 94 cm
Signed and dated at lower left on the pedestal
of the lion: Eques de Lampi / pinxit ao. 1806.
Inv. no. GE 356
Provenance: commissioned in Vienna in 1806
by Prince Andreas Kirillowitsch Rasumofsky;
acquired in 1837 from the estate of Prince
Rasumofsky by Prince Alois II von Liechtenstein

II.6 / p. 81
Friedrich von Amerling (1803–87)
Portrait of the Sculptor Bertel Thorvaldsen
(1770–1844), 1843
Oil on canvas, 103 x 81 cm
Signed and dated at lower left: F. Amerling 1843
Signed, above this, by the sitter: Thorvaldsen
Inv. no. GE 353
Provenance: acquired in 1845 from Amerling
by Prince Alois II von Liechtenstein

II.7 / p. 82
Antonio Canova (1757–1822)
Bust of Napoleon Francis, King of Rome
(1811–32), 1812
Marble, height 50 cm
Signed and dated on the back of the pedestal:
Roi de Rome / MDCCCXII / Canova. /FECIT
Inv. no. SK 623
Provenance: gift from August Ignaz von Liechten-
stein to Prince Johann II von Liechtenstein

II.8 / p. 83
Studio of Antonio Canova (1757–1822)
Bust of Napoleon I, Emperor of France
(1769–1821), early 19th century
Marble, height 68 cm
Signed on the front: NAPOLEON
Inscription on the back: 96
Inv. no. SK 622
Provenance: acquired by Prince Johann II
von Liechtenstein

II.9 / p. 85
Anonymous, Austrian
Bust of Pallas Athena, late 18th century
Marble, height 70 cm
Inv. no, SK 615

II.10 / p. 84
Pietro Tenerani (1798–1869)
Bust of a Girl, 1837
Marble, height 52 cm
Signed and dated on the back: P. Tenerani F. 1837
Inv. no. SK 643
Provenance: probably acquired by Prince Alois II
von Liechtenstein; recorded in 1841 in the
conservatory of the palace of Prince Rasumofsky
in Vienna in 1841

II.11 / pp. 86–87
Johann Peter Krafft (1780–1856)
Archduke Karl (1771–1847) *with his Staff*
at the Battle of Aspern, 1820
Oil on canvas, 112 x 159 cm
Signed and dated at lower right: PKrafft.pinx 1820
Inv. no. GE 1873
Provenance: commissioned in 1821 by Prince
Johann I von Liechtenstein

II.12 / p. 88
Giovanni Battista Lampi (1751–1830)
Portrait of Prince Johann I von Liechtenstein
(1760–1836), 1816
Oil on canvas, 80 x 64 cm
Inv. no. GE 465
Provenance: commissioned in 1816 by Prince
Johann I von Liechtenstein

II.13 / p. 89
Peter Eduard Ströhling (1768–after 1826)
Portrait of Prince Alois I von Liechtenstein
(1759–1805), 1794
Oil on canvas, 82 x 66 cm
Inv. no. GE 1535
Provenance: acquired in 1794 by Prince Alois I
von Liechtenstein

II.14 / p. 90
Friedrich Oelenhainz (1745–1804)
Portrait of the Future Prince Johann I
von Liechtenstein (1760–1836), 1776
Oil on canvas, 105 x 142 cm
Inv. no. GE 1758, companion piece to inv. nos.
GE 1756, GE 1757, and GE 1760
Provenance: commissioned in 1776, along with
seven further family portraits, by Prince Franz
Josef I von Liechtenstein; until 1944 in the
'Family Room' of the manor house at Eisgrub

II.15 / p. 90
Friedrich Oelenhainz (1745–1804)
Portrait of the Future Prince Alois I von Liechten-
stein (1759–1805), 1776
Oil on canvas, 104 x 143 cm
Inv. no. GE 1757, companion piece to inv. nos.
GE 1756, GE 1758, and GE 1760
Provenance: commissioned in 1776, along with
seven further family portraits, by Prince Franz
Josef I von Liechtenstein; until 1944 in the
'Family Room' of the manor house at Eisgrub

II.16 / p. 92
Friedrich Oelenhainz (1745–1804)
Portrait of Princess Leopoldine Adelgunde von
Liechtenstein (1754–1823), 1776
Oil on canvas, 105 x 143 cm
Inv. no. GE 1756, companion piece to inv. nos.
GE 1757, GE 1758, and GE 1760
Provenance: commissioned in 1776, along with
seven further family portraits, by Prince Franz
Josef I von Liechtenstein; until 1944 in the
'Family Room' of the manor house at Eisgrub

II.17 / p. 93
Friedrich Oelenhainz (1745–1804)
Portrait of Princess Maria Josepha Hermenegilde
von Liechtenstein (1768–1845), 1776
Oil on canvas, 102 x 142 cm
Inv. no. GE 1760, companion piece to inv. nos.
GE 1756, GE 1757, and GE 1758
Provenance: commissioned in 1776, along with
seven further family portraits, by Prince Franz
Josef I von Liechtenstein; until 1944 in the
'Family Room' of the manor house at Eisgrub

II.18 / p. 94
Elisabeth Vigée-Lebrun (1755–1842)
Portrait of Princess Karoline von Liechtenstein, née
Countess von Manderscheit (1768–1831), as Iris,
1793
Oil on canvas, 222 x 159 cm
Signed and dated: L.E. Vigée Lebrun à Vienne.
1793
Inv. no. GE 1787, companion piece to inv. no.
GE 1786
Provenance: commissioned in 1794, along with
the *Portrait of Princess Maria Jospeha*
Hermenegilde von Liechtenstein, later Princess
Esterházy, as Ariadne on Naxos (inv. no. GE 1786),
by Prince Alois I von Liechtenstein; originally part
of the decoration of the Liechtenstein palace in
Herrengasse, Vienna

II.19 / p. 95
Elisabeth Vigée-Lebrun (1755–1842)
Portrait of Princess Maria Josepha Hermenegilde
von Liechtenstein, later Princess Esterházy
(1768–1845), as Ariadne on Naxos, 1793
Oil on canvas, 221 x 159 cm
Signed and dated: L.E. Vigée Lebrun à Vienne
1793
Inv. no. GE 1786, companion piece to inv. no.
GE 1787
Provenance: commissioned in 1794, along with
the *Portrait of Princess Karoline von Liechtenstein,*
née Countess von Manderscheit, as Iris (inv. no.
GE 1787), by Prince Alois I von Liechtenstein;
originally part of the decoration of the Liechtenstein palace in Herrengasse, Vienna

II.20 / p. 96
Giovanni Battista Lampi (1755–1830)
Portrait Sketch of Princess Josepha Sophie von
Liechtenstein, née Countess zu Fürstenberg-Weitra
(1776–1848)
Oil on canvas, 37 x 30 cm
Inv.no. GE 1222
Provenance: probably acquired by Prince Johann I
von Liechtenstein

II.21 / p. 99
Angelica Kauffmann (1741–1807)
Sketch for the *Portrait of Ferdinand IV, King of*
Naples and both Sicily (1759–1825) and his
Family, 1782 (final composition in the Museo di
Capodimonte, Naples)
Pen and brown ink with brown and grey wash
over black chalk on paper, 23 x 30 cm
Inv. no. GR 522
Provenance: acquired in 1983 by Prince Josef II
von and zu Liechtenstein

II.22 / p. 97
Angelica Kauffmann (1741–1807)
Modello for the *Portrait of Ferdinand IV, King*
of Naples and both Sicily (1759–1825) and his
Family, 1782/83
(final composition in the Museo di Capodimonte,
Naples)
Signed at left on the base of the steps: A.K. pinx.
Inv. no. GE 2070
Provenance: first recorded in the Princely
Collections in 1910

II.23 / p. 100
Anton Hickel (1745–98)
Portrait of Marie-Thérèse, Princesse de Lamballe
(1749–92), 1788
Oil on canvas, 66 x 44 cm
Signed and dated at lower right: hickel 1788
Inv. no. GE 1675
Provenance: first recorded in the Princely
Collections in 1899

II.24 / pp. 102–03
Heinrich von Füger (1751–1818)
Prometheus Brings Fire to Mankind, 1817
Oil on canvas, 221 x 156 cm
Inv. no. GE 1362
Provenance: acquired in 1823 by Prince Johann I
von Liechtenstein at the Viennese auction of the
collection of Prince Prosper von Sinzendorf

II.25 / p. 104
Franz Anton Zauner (1746–1822)
Nymph with a Putto, Figures for a Fountain
(probably intended for the fountain in the courtyard
of the palace at Neulengbach), after 1797
Lead-tin alloy, height 112 cm, width 235 cm,
depth 90 cm
Inv. no. SK 1408
Provenance: probably acquired in 1797 by Count
Johann von Fries; sold in 1823, together with
Schloss Neulengbach, to Prince Johann I von
Liechtenstein; recorded in 1822 in the library
of the Liechtenstein Garden Palace at Rossau;
from 1933 on the island in the lake of the garden
of the palace at Rossau

II.26 / p. 105
Johann Martin Fischer (1740–1820)
The Dream of St Joseph (second version of a
relief for the *Josef Fountain* in the Graben, Vienna),
c. 1804
Lead-tin alloy, height 99 cm, width 69 cm
Inv. no. SK 907
Provenance: acquired in 2002 by Prince
Hans-Adam II von und zu Liechtenstein

II.27 / p. 106
Ascribed to Franz Xaver Messerschmidt
(1736–83)
Bust of a Man, *c.* 1770
Lead-tin alloy, silver-plated, height 40 cm
Private collection, Vienna

II.28 / p. 107
Joseph Hardtmuth (1758–1816), design
Two panels for the decoration of the Liechtenstein
palace in Herrengasse, Vienna, *c.* 1792
Painted and gilded wood, height 160 cm, width
62 cm; height 167 cm, width 69 cm
Inv. nos. MO 1578 and MO 1579
Provenance: in the Liechtenstein palace in
Herrengasse, Vienna; after 1913 in storage

II.29 / p. 108
Joseph Hardtmuth (1758–1816), design
Candelabrum with girandole (from an original
series of eight, probably made for the decoration
of the Liechtenstein palace in Herrengasse,
Vienna), *c.* 1790
Carved and gilded linewood, gilt bronze,
height 185 cm each
Inv. no. SK 23
Provenance: in the Liechtenstein palace in Herren-
gasse, Vienna; in 1920 recorded in the Hercules
Room of the Liechtenstein Garden Palace at
Rossau

II.30 / p. 109
Anonymous, Genoese
Console table, late 18th century
Wood, marble (table top), height 101 cm,
width 124 cm, depth 56 cm
Inv. no. MO 1563
Provenance: acquired in 2003 by Prince
Hans-Adam II von und zu Liechtenstein at auction
at Sotheby's, London

GALLERY III

THE WORLD OF BIEDERMEIER

After the terrors of the Napoleonic Wars and the political re-ordering of Europe at the Congress of Vienna, there was a widespread longing for a sunnier and more tranquil world. And, just as it was said that 'the Congress danced', exuberantly celebrating the achievement of a society at peace, so too, in the private sphere, and after nearly a generation of war and enmity that had claimed so many lives, there was a desire to have done for a while with an interest in politics. It was once again possible to travel unimpeded and therefore to get to know foreign countries. And excellent use was made of this opportunity, not least by painters, who once more made their way from the north to the south of Europe, now responding above all to the sheer quality of the southern light.

Much as the northern European artists of this period were fond of their native regions and, for the most part, evolved their skills in relation to the cultural context in which they lived (where their subjects might be the Vienna Woods, limestone outcrops, or the mountains), they nonetheless found that journeying to the south of Europe freed them from the physical and intellectual confinement to which they had become accustomed. The lure of the South proved to be remarkably strong, and one can really feel and breathe the southern air in the paintings produced there. Artists such as Ferdinand Georg Waldmüller (1793–1865) and Rudolf von Alt (1812–1905) seized on the rich colouring of the southern light, noticing how it in turn revealed a quite different range of colours in the landscape. They analysed the distinct moods or atmospheres brought about by conditions found only in the South: occasions when the light was astonishingly pure and clear or, on the contrary, when there was a dense haze. They observed the strong, steady light of the morning and the evening, of which nothing even remotely comparable is to be found in a mountain landscape, where the sun rises and sets without invoking such chromatic extremes. Then, when they had had enough of their travels, the artists brought the light of the South back home with them: Waldmüller's paintings of the landscape of the Hinterbrühl would not have been bathed in such a golden light had the artist not himself previously experienced such light in Italy. It is well known that one sees only what one already knows. By the same token, the uncompromising light of the South led artists very rapidly to see and to understand new things, things that they had not encountered in the same form in the North. For the first time, Waldmüller went out into the landscape and sketched with great intensity, both noting what he saw and even making one or two rapid, cursory paintings en plein air.

Artists also learnt how to circumvent the extremes of light, not only when painting landscapes but also in rendering interiors. Here, they would articulate light by painting the traces that it left behind as it penetrated a room: they were thereby able to capture the mood and atmosphere of a particular space. (Painters had in fact for some time been concerned with conveying more than the mere objective appearance of the physical world.) Moreover, along with an interest in the nature of light came a fascination with the character of the weather, and the resulting attempt to capture the essence of storms, lightning, and thunder, as well as all manner of natural catastrophes. Painters went as far as it was then possible to go in recording the natural world, being eager to plumb the depths of their abilities, to test the power of their imaginations, and, moreover, to give the spectator a sense of his or her immediate involvement in the depicted scene. By this means, there evolved a pictorial world that was thematically far removed from that of the era of the Baroque. Painters no longer needed to look for their subjects to another realm – be it that of the Bible or of Antiquity. Rather, they consulted their own experience: what they had themselves seen and felt. The world as directly observed and spontaneously imagined by the individual now displaced the old concern with reference to a supposedly objective reality. Seemingly insignificant things were now observed and recorded, often being drawn and painted with painstaking care. Artists also began to explore the 'world within' and then to make the fruits of this inner journey accessible to others.

In Joseph Rebell's (1787–1828) The Eruption of Vesuvius at Night, one can sense how his inner being must have trembled with excitement at this blending of water and fire. The sheer profusion of colours that the artist has hurled at his canvas is itself enough to tell us something of his inner state while observing this natural phenomenon. The gleam of the brightly moonlit sky competes with the glow of the molten lava tumbling down the mountain into the sea. Even earlier, Rebell's teacher, Michael Wutky of Krems (1739–1822), had embarked on capturing similar moods, repeatedly taking Vesuvius and its environs as his theme. Jacob Philipp Hackert (1737–1807) had also treated this subject, although approaching it in a manner that was much more academic and tentative, and altogether lacking in the freedom that Rebell achieves in his own picture. In the present work Rebell is notable, above all, for his audacity: his record of a veritable inferno is visionary, conveying not a sense of fear but a sort of ecstasy.

It is, however, precisely the opposite that we find in the case of Rebell's *View of Atrani on the Gulf of Salerno*: a peaceful landscape bathed in the soft light of the South, a seemingly inner light that illuminates landscape, architecture, and staffage, here consisting of boats with fishermen in the foreground. The sense of serenity is assured by what is absent as much as by what we are shown: no turbulent ocean but an almost mirror-smooth sea, no jagged rocks but a compact little town nestling under a cliff and a softly modelled hill in the background. The mood is, indeed, almost contemplative, taking its cue from the illumination of the early morning, before the stark contrast of bright light and shade has emerged owing to the sun's harsh rays.

Rebell spent many years in, or *en route* to, Italy (in 1809 he was in Switzerland, in 1810/11 in Milan, in 1813–15 in Naples, and in 1816–24 in Rome) before becoming Director of the Imperial Picture Gallery, at that time housed in the Belvedere Palace in Vienna. As a marine painter, he followed in the footsteps of Claude-Joseph Vernet (1714–89), who had 'discovered' the landscape of the Neapolitan coast as a subject for artists, thereby establishing it as an alternative to the Roman *campagna*.

JOSEF REBELL 1787–1828
View of Atrani on the Gulf of Salerno, 1822
III.2

Thomas Ender (1793–1875), who had travelled to Italy in 1819 as a draughtsman in the retinue of the Austrian Emperor Franz I and had then stayed on, as the recipient of a stipend, until 1822, met and came to know his fellow painter Joseph Rebell in Rome. Ender then travelled south and devoted himself, with great success, to painting the Bay of Naples, and of course the city itself, at the base of Mount Vesuvius, though also turning his attention to other picturesque spots nearby, including Salerno, Sorrento, Amalfi and the island of Capri. From a letter sent by Ender to the Viennese art dealer Artaria, we learn how passionately he saw Italy as his mentor: '[…] in those days in Vienna I had not yet seen a sunny sky, now it is my sole endeavour to imitate this. I have firmly resolved that as long as I remain in Italy

THOMAS ENDER 1793–1875
The Gulf of Sorrento
III.3

I shall do everything possible to study the effect of aerial perspective on colour [...]'. In his *Gulf of Sorrento*, Ender depicts one of the most beautiful landscapes in the world, one of the most dramatic stretches of coastline, where nature and the hand of man complement each other in an extraordinary and delightful fashion. Ender's view shows the entire panorama from the breathtakingly steep coast to the calm plain in the background, from which Vesuvius rises. Here, Ender uses aerial perspective to create a sense of endless distance, capturing both the sky of the South and the incomparable colour of the sea in the Gulf of Naples. He returned from Italy to Vienna with over five hundred

drawings and around forty smaller and six larger oil paintings. After Rudolf von Alt, Ender was the quintessential *vedutista* of Viennese Biedermeier. His skills, both in oils and in painstakingly executed watercolours, were repeatedly in evidence both at home and, yet again, abroad – even as far away as Brazil. Numerous works by Rudolf von Alt and Thomas Ender, produced both in Italy and in the Austrian Crownlands, are to be found in the Princely Collections. The estates and properties of the House of Liechtenstein were recorded above all in the enchanting views and interiors painted by Rudolf von Alt.

FERDINAND GEORG WALDMÜLLER 1793–1865
The Ruins of the Greek Theatre at Taormina on Sicily, 1844
III.4

The highpoint of the engagement of Austrian painters with the light of the South was, without doubt, to be found in the work of the aforementioned Ferdinand Georg Waldmüller, whose views of the ancient temples in Sicily are among the most striking ever to be painted by a northern artist working under the southern sun. From 1825 onwards, Waldmüller spent the summer of almost every year in Italy, and in 1841 he travelled for the first time to Sicily, thereafter continuing to visit the island. In his autobiography, written in 1847, Waldmüller observed: 'In order to add to my experiences, I repeatedly travelled to Italy, extending my itinerary to include Sicily, where for a couple of years I devoted my vacations to fervent study.'

Waldmüller made good use of these stays in Sicily, learning how to capture the stunning impact of the southern light on the landscape. Unlike Rebell and Ender, he did not record the light as merely indifferent or with strong chiaroscuro effects. His landscapes are, rather, bathed in glistening sunlight, and a golden glow covers all three views to be found in the Princely Collections: *The Ruins of the Greek Theatre at Taormina on Sicily*, *The Temple of Juno Lacinia at Agrigento*, and *The Temple of Concord at Agrigento*. Here, Waldmüller paints the parched landscapes of summer, where everything is burnt to shades of yellow, the only contrast being provided by the green of the cacti and the almost silvery gleam of the foliage of the olive trees. The light also envelops the architectural elements in each scene, even the red tile roofs losing their distinctive brightness.

FERDINAND GEORG WALDMÜLLER 1793–1865

The Ruins of the Temple of Juno Lacinia at Agrigento, *c.* 1845

III.5

In Waldmüller's view of Taormina he lays out before us the stage scenery of the ancient theatre. It is stage scenery in a double sense, for behind the ruins of the original stage wall there unfolds the most beautiful of all possible stage sets: the Gulf of Taormina with Mount Etna gently rising in the background, a small plume of smoke ascending from its crater and merging with the sky. In Waldmüller's view of the Temple of Juno Lacinia he remains true to the demands of his own treatise of 1846: 'that the colouring in the case of a real work of art should appear a secondary consideration, the principal concern being the persuasive record of light and shade.' We recognise this light from the South through its effects: it exaggerates the outlines of every form and seems to bring almost within our grasp the motifs

we observe in the distance, such as the trees of the olive grove and the temple itself. It is a light that heightens the sense of three-dimensionality while limiting chromatic differentiation to a few tones: the yellows of the burnt meadow contrasting with the nuanced silvery gleam of the foliage of the olive trees. The ruined temple stands majestically on its acropolis in sharply raking light. It has taken on the colour of this light, but is set off against the surrounding sky by its sharply shaded edges. The view of the Temple of Concord is sketchier in character and less thoroughly worked than the two others. It shows

the almost fully preserved structure from above, as if it were an integral part of the barren coastal plain.

For the Austrian artists of these years Italy resembled an experimental laboratory. And just as varied as their Italian destinations was that which they brought back with them from the South to Vienna. As became apparent after their return, each was influenced and marked by Italy according to his own character and concerns.

Waldmüller retained his fondness for extreme light conditions even in the landscapes that he painted in the Salzkammergut and, above all,

FERDINAND GEORG WALDMÜLLER 1793–1865

The Temple of Concord at Agrigento, 1849

III.6

in the environs of Vienna. According to a review of the Waldmüller memorial retrospective mounted in 1866 by his former pupils: 'His secret must, not least, have lain in the fact that he painted *en plein air*, a practice that in those days met with almost universal incomprehension. It was said that he discovered in his old age that, in order to obtain truly glowing colour, one had to paint in sunlight. This would

seem to account for the curiously glaring colour in many of the paintings of his last years […].' Thirty years after his death Waldmüller was regarded by the Viennese Secessionists as their own forerunner, on account of his *plein-airisme*. In 1898 their supporter Hermann Bahr observed of Waldmüller: 'What power, what life, what sun! Nowhere here do we find the gloom of the academy; how it all dazzles!

RUDOLF VON ALT 1812–1905
The Piazza del Duomo in Como
III.7

RUDOLF VON ALT 1812–1905

View of Naples

III.8

FERDINAND GEORG WALDMÜLLER 1793–1865
Mountain Landscape with the Ruin of Liechtenstein near Mödling, 1859
III.9

Back then he already knew what air was! We are astonished, simply cannot comprehend it, when we recall exactly how long ago it was that he was living and painting […].'
Waldmüller's innovations, his glistening light and glaring colour, are to be found at their strongest in his *Mountain Landscape with the Ruin of Liechtenstein near Mödling*, painted in 1859. This picture shows the centre of the artificial landscape with fantastical architectural elements

laid out by the Liechtenstein family after they had re-acquired the site of their ancestral home in 1806. This was rapidly transformed after the model of an English landscape garden, and artificial ruins, an amphitheatre, the Hussars' Temple and other such structures were erected. As in the case of his Sicilian landscapes, Waldmüller shows his subject an uncharitably dazzling and harsh light, but the intensity lessens towards the background, where billowing smoke envelops the

FERDINAND GEORG WALDMÜLLER 1793–1865
View of Mödling, 1848
III.10

landscape in a soft, subdued light. Waldmüller here effectively blends the harsh light of his Sicilian landscapes with the *sfumato* effect of aerial perspective that is subtly suggestive of atmosphere. In Waldmüller's *View of Mödling*, painted a decade earlier, the treatment of light is much less extreme, even though this picture is unthinkable without the artist's earlier experience of Italy. Here, too, he evolves a form of aerial perspective. This takes its starting point in the foreground with the garishly lit peasant woman seeking rest; it then embraces the lively modelling of the foliage; and it ends with the soaring spire of the Spitalskirche and the former textile factory. In the far distance we see the Park of Laxenburg and the framing band of the Leitha Hills. For all its topographical accuracy, Waldmüller's

FERDINAND GEORG WALDMÜLLER 1793–1865

Lime-kiln in the Hinterbrühl, *c.* 1845

III.11

FERDINAND GEORG WALDMÜLLER 1793–1865
Lake Fuschl with the Schafberg, *c.* 1835
III.12

View of Mödling provides only a fleeting impression of the observed scene, being focused on the atmosphere evoked by particular lighting conditions. We sense that in the very next moment the interrelationships of colour and light may have altered, resulting in an utterly different effect of aerial perspective and a new interrelationship of the various 'strata' of the landscape – and hence a quite different picture. Thomas Ender's *glacier landscape* shows us the icy light of the Alps. Since 1829 Ender had been one of the painters attached to the court of Archduke Johann of Austria. Alongside his colleagues Rudolf von Alt,

Gurk and Loder, he recorded landscapes and rural genre scenes in hundreds of watercolours. His works and the *vedute* of Rudolf von Alt are among the most impressive testaments to the Austrian contribution to this subtle art. Here, Ender depicts a hiker who has ascended into the upper reaches of the mountains and finds himself high up between the peaks, where he is suddenly dwarfed by the barrier formed by the gigantic tongue of a glacier. Ender's watercolours and oil paintings typically record their observed subjects in such detail that they convey an impression of enormous density.

THOMAS ENDER 1793–1875
The Vogelmaier Ochsenkar Kees in the Rauris Valley
in the High Tauern, 1834
III.13

Friedrich Gauermann (1807–62), in *The Harvest Wagon* of 1837, is interested not in the overwhelming, lonely world of the upper mountain slopes, but in a painstakingly rendered scene in which every detail contributes to the setting. In the book in which he recorded his income and expenditure, Gauermann provides the following brief description of this painting: 'A wagon, laden with corn, is being driven swiftly up a hill; it is pulled with great effort by two horses, one white and one chest-nut; the former is ridden by a lad who is goading it on; a third horse has been harnessed separately from the two others and is being led by a young boy. On the hill lying to the left there are trees bent by the wind, with a farmhouse in their shade. A storm is rolling in across the high mountain peaks in the background; in the middle distance lies Lake Zeller; a great many countryfolk are also making their way up the hill; the wind had whisked a boy's hat off his head, and two men

FRIEDRICH GAUERMANN 1807–62

The Harvest Wagon, 1837

III.14

have come to a stop by the wagon.' It is, above all, the rising storm and the dramatic, cloudy sky that have provoked the critical situation depicted by Gauermann: the wagon heaped with golden hay still has to be carried home, the horses press on in dragging it up the hill, the mounted boy urging them on with cracks of his whip. But the path is still dry, for dust swirls around beneath the horses' hooves. The farm dog accompanies the beasts, darting nimbly back and forth, and behind the hay wagon the weary harvest helpers make their way home. Gauermann renders each and every detail with extraordinary clarity.

FRIEDRICH VON AMERLING 1803–87

Portrait of Princess Marie Franziska von Liechtenstein (1834–1909) at the Age of Two, 1836

III.15

Detail

III.16

In the Biedermeier period portraiture was just as important as landscape painting. The two major portraitists of this period were stylistic opposites: Ferdinand Georg Waldmüller (whom we already know as a landscapist) and Friedrich von Amerling (1803–87). Both are well represented in the Princely Collections.

Like no other Viennese painter of the Biedermeier Era, Amerling was able to capture and convey the humanity of his sitters in his portraits of them. Whether in images of children or in his record of the faces of the young or old, he always rendered the sitter's character with an astonishing impartiality and a directness that sufficed to remove every sense of a barrier between the subject and the spectator.

Prince Alois II von Liechtenstein commissioned Amerling to paint his children. The result was a touching series of portraits of Marie Franziska (painted in 1836), Karoline (in 1837), Sophie (in 1838), and, finally, the five-year-old heir to the title, Johann (in 1844/45). The

sleepy two-year-old Princess Marie Franziska is, without doubt, the strongest portrait of the series: smiling happily to herself, the sleepy child firmly clutches a doll. The spectator looks at her as if looking down on her from above, and the sunlight falling gently across her hair brings out the colour in her cheeks. Here, too, as in the landscape painting we have considered, it is the artist's observation of the moment, his record of the smallest details, and his success in capturing the atmosphere established by light that ensure the creation of a work of art out of the depiction of a series of seemingly peripheral details. Princess Karoline von Liechtenstein appears to challenge the spectator with her gaze, as if perhaps annoyed by our approach – or does she merely seek to make an impression with her glance? She, too, is sketched with the sort of brisk brushstroke at which Amerling excelled. Equally exquisite is the portrait of Princess Sophie von Liechtenstein, her softly modelled face concluding this trio of female portraits.

FRIEDRICH VON AMERLING 1803–87
Portrait of Princess Karoline von Liechtenstein (1836–85)
at the Age of One and a Half, 1837
III.16

FRIEDRICH VON AMERLING 1803–87
Portrait of Princess Sophie von Liechtenstein (1837–99)
at the Age of about One and a Half, 1838
III.17

FRIEDRICH VON AMERLING 1803–87

Oil sketch for the Portrait of the Future Prince Johann II
von Liechtenstein (1840–1929) on a White Pony, 1844/45
III.18

FRIEDRICH VON AMERLING 1803–87

Portrait of the Future Prince Johann II von Liechtenstein (1840–
1929) on a White Pony, 1845
III.19

It was followed by the striking sketch of the five-year-old Johann von
Liechtenstein (1840–1929), the future Prince Johann II, on his white
pony. Amerling has here captured the striking vivacity of his subjects.
In this little masterpiece we can sense how direct the relationship
between the painter and his subject must have been, and we can see
how Amerling was able to draw on this relative intimacy in painting his
portrait. Quite distinct in character, however, is the large finished painting derived from this sketch, with its oppulent frame, made for the
rooms of the palace in Bankgasse, which had recently been re-decorated

in a Neo-Rococo style. The pony, so lively in the sketch, is as if 'frozen' in
the painting, while the child now seems to sit stiffly in the saddle. Evidently, Amerling had too little experience in adapting his record of the
sitter to the requirements of a painting on such a scale. Used to capturing the intimate, he failed to live up to the demands of this commission.
By contrast, portraits of the Liechtenstein children made even in the
Neoclassical period – *Portrait of Princess Ida Leopoldine and Prince
Rudolf von Liechtenstein* (respectively, 1811–84 and 1816–48) or
Portrait of Prince Franz de Paula and Prince Karl Johann von

UNKNOWN ARTIST IN THE CIRCLE OF HEINRICH VON FÜGER 1751–1818

Portrait of the Children of Prince Johann I von Liechtenstein: Princess Ida Leopoldine
(1811–84) and Prince Rudolf (1816–48), *c.* 1820

III.20

UNKNOWN ARTIST IN THE CIRCLE OF HEINRICH VON FÜGER 1751–1818

Portrait of the Sons of Prince Johann I von Liechtenstein: Prince Franz de Paula
(1802–87) and Prince Karl Johann (1803–71), *c.* 1815

III.21

Liechtenstein (respectively, 1802–87 and 1803–71), children of Prince Johann I – seem fresh and alive and show their subjects unself-consciously playing in landscape settings or engaged in looking at drawings. It goes without saying that these images are imbued with a sense of composure: for all their naturalness, the four children are nonetheless posing for the spectator. These portraits have traditionally been ascribed to Heinrich von Füger.

Ferdinand Georg Waldmüller's 1832 image of the two-year-old Franz Josef, the future Austrian Emperor (1830–1916, r. 1848–1916), pos-ing for the artist in the uniform of a grenadier and equipped with a set of similarly dressed Hungarian wooden figures, strikes us as a state portrait in miniature. The child looks out at the world with his seeming-ly innocent blue eyes almost as if he really had nothing at all to do with the setting that was later to surround him as a monarch. Yet, even at this early stage of his life, the future Austrian Emperor has hit upon what was to become the military career that was to prove so calami-tous for the Austro-Hungarian Monarchy.

FEDINAND GEORG WALDMÜLLER 1793–1865

Portrait of the Future Emperor Franz Josef I of Austria (1830–1916) as a Grenadier with Toy Soldiers, 1832

III.22

The significance of Waldmüller as a portraitist is revealed by two male portraits in which the painter was able to characterise his sitters with quite astonishing accuracy. His superb *Portrait of Thiery, Landlord of the Wolf-in-the-Meadow Inn*, painted in 1833, goes quite beyond the usual Biedermeier standard of objectivity tempered by engagement in its directness, and sketches a living soul with as much vivacity as exactitude. The innkeeper appears to regard the spectator in a spirit of scepticism, maintaining a self-confident distance from his interlocutor. Portraits such as this and the one of Charles de Moreau are in every respect the equal of those painted at this period by Jean-Auguste-Dominique Ingres (1780–1867) or by Jacques-Louis David (1748–1825).

In Waldmüller's 1822 portrait of *Portrait of the Architect Charles de Moreau* (1758–1841), we have a record of one of the most important architects of the age, who was responsible, above all, for the building projects undertaken by the Esterházy family, to whom the Liechtensteins were at this time closely related. Moreau was the architect of the planned, albeit only partly executed, re-building of the palace at Eisenstadt, where the aim was to create a truly princely residence complete with library and theatre. Posed frontally, the sitter looks directly at the spectator, in a manner that seems to reflect his style as an architect, which was characterised by a certain rigidity and severity. At the same time, we do not feel that we are here encountering a closed and secretive face; its seeming openness invites us, even challenges us, to engage in dialogue.

A 'portrait of the artist' of a quite different type was made by Friedrich von Amerling in 1833, when he took as his subject his fellow painter Peter Fendi. Amerling uses loose brushstrokes to capture an impression of the sitter's head, but the clothes and background are only roughly indicated. This portrait is not at all intended as an imposing record. By comparison with the portraits painted by Waldmüller, its dynamism is especially striking. This is also true of Amerling's *Study of the Head of a Bearded Man*, whose characterful face, with its prominent eyes, glows vividly against an almost black background. It, too, shows a lively and approachable person, such as we feel we might really meet. In his *Self-portrait*, meanwhile, Amerling has preserved for posterity an image of himself in profile. We know of twenty-seven such self-portraits, in each of which Amerling shows us a different aspect of himself.

FERDINAND GEORG WALDMÜLLER 1793–1865

Portrait of the Architect Charles de Moreau (1758–1841), 1822

III.24

FRIEDRICH VON AMERLING 1803–87
Portrait of the Painter Peter Fendi (1796–1842), 1833
III.25

FRIEDRICH VON AMERLING 1803–87
Study of the Head of a Bearded Man
III.26

FRIEDRICH VON AMERLING 1803–87
Self-portrait, 1844
III.27

FRIEDRICH VON AMERLING 1803–87
Self-portrait, 1844
III.27

FRANZ EYBL 1806–80
Portrait of the Surgeon Josef Walz
III.28

FRANZ EYBL 1806–80
Berry Picker before a Mountain, 1844
III.29

Not at all unlike Amerling's portraits, be it in the overall painterly character or in the use of loose, cursory brushstrokes to capture a general impression of the sitter, is the *Portrait of the Surgeon Josef Walz* by Franz Eybl (1806–80). In modelling the face, Eybl demonstrates a masterly control of illumination and the most refined use of nuance. Eybl's *Berry Picker before a Mountain* of 1844 shows a peasant girl against an imposing mountain landscape. Here, too, he provides a delicately nuanced rendering of the face, and he demonstrates his skill in particular in his treatment of the varieties of surface texture, especially that of the clothing. The red scarf with its pattern, the colourful bodice visible below it, the blue apron, and the white of the blouse, and finally the scarf worn on the head constitute a composition in themselves. The girl does not direct her gaze at the spectator; rather, as if in pensive mood, she seems deep in contemplation. She thereby introduces an almost meditative calm into the picture.

This element of contemplation is also to be found in Amerling's picture of around 1835, *Lost in her Dreams*, and his comparable *Portrait of Elise Kreuzberger* of 1837. In neither picture does Amerling seek the illusion of direct eye contact between sitter and spectator. Elise Kreuzberger turns her gaze away, just as the brownish-green eyes of the girl absorbed in dreams appear to gaze into the depths of her own being or into the uncharted distance. In both paintings the modelling of the flesh tones is extremely refined. And the treatment of the diverse textures of the materials featured in the clothing contributes significantly to the charm of both pictures. The veils and the fur are each so skilfully rendered as to seem almost tangible.

FRIEDRICH VON AMERLING 1803–87
Portrait of Elise Kreuzberger, 1837
III.31

FRIEDRICH VON AMERLING 1803–87
Lost in her Dreams, *c.* 1835
III.30

FRANCESCO HAYEZ 1791–1882
Vengeance is Sworn, 1852
III.32

Francesco Hayez (1791–1882), of whom a fine portrait by Friedrich von Amerling is preserved in a private collection in Milan, painted the striking picture of 1852, *Vengeance is Sworn*. The composition is dominated by the two almost life-size figures at its centre, their detailed treatment set off by the very summary background with its suggestion of Venetian palaces and a fountain. Hayez, too, was a master of the rendering of the distinct qualities of diverse types of cloth, from the flowered pattern of the dress, by way of the gleam of the silk, to the transparency of the veil.

Hayez was intimately connected with the Viennese art world of this period. He had arrived in Vienna in 1836 in order to contribute to the process of reform then underway at the Academy of Fine Arts, and he was presented to the Emperor by Prince Metternich. Viennese painters of this period were also attentive to developments elsewhere in Europe; and awareness of what was being painted in England, in France, and in Italy ensured a certain openness that was to find its reflection in the work produced in Vienna. It is by reference to the art produced at this period in these other countries that we are able to make meaningful comparisons. Such broad reference supplies us with the criteria that allow us to recognise the significance and the quality of the painting of the Biedermeier Era in Vienna, even by the standards established by this international context.

FRANZ VON LENBACH 1836–1904

Portrait of the Architect Gottfried Semper (1803–79)

III.33

Of particular note, in conclusion, are the two pictures by Franz von Lenbach (1836–1904) displayed in this room: a fleetingly sketchy *Portrait of the Architect Gottfried Semper* (1803–79), painted shortly before the sitter's death, and *Portrait of Prince Rudolf von Liechtenstein* (1833–88), dated 1886. Both portraits omit everything that might be understood to allude to the status and the social significance of their subjects, the focus being on their intriguing faces, which are captured in vigorous, loose brushstrokes. Dispensing with the external, the painter was here able to achieve an image that reflected in some measure the innermost soul of his sitters.

FRANZ VON LENBACH 1836–1904

Portrait of Prince Rudolf von Liechtenstein (1833–88), 1886

III.34

JOSEPH NIGG 1782–1863
Floral Still Life with White Grapes, 1838
III.35

JOSEPH NIGG 1782–1863

Floral Still Life with Black Grapes, 1838

III.36

Of special importance in the display in this room are the examples of porcelain. It has nowadays almost been forgotten that the Liechtenstein family could also lay claim to one of the most important collections of porcelain in existence, and was among the earliest customers of Du Paquier, the first Viennese porcelain maker and internationally regarded as second only to Meissen. In those days these rare pieces of refinement were seen as being in the vanguard of both art and design. The Princely Collections, in particular on account of important recent acquisitions, are also impressively rich in products of the next important era in Viennese porcelain production, that associated with Sorgenthal. It is, indeed, not at all surprising that this should be so at a time when architecture and the applied arts were virtually dominated by commissions issued by the Liechtenstein family. Sorgenthal porcelain, with its clear forms and its strong colours, is as perfect an encapsulation of the taste of the period as is its equivalent in architecture and painting. The examples to be found in the Princely Collections are intended for show and were never used. Their state of preservation is, accordingly, outstanding.

Among the most valuable items of this kind in the Princely Collections are two splendid decorative plaques made in 1838 by Joseph Nigg (1782–1863), recently acquired from a private collection. Nigg was probably the most important porcelain painter then active in Vienna. His work constituted the simultaneous continuation and adaptation of Dutch floral still-life painting, which in Vienna had been taken up by Waldmüller and others. These plaques are also among the most technically brilliant pieces of porcelain to be produced in Vienna. They were especially favoured as gifts in diplomatic circles and they found their way into the art collections of the time. The fact that there was a special class for instruction in flower painting at the Viennese porcelain factory testifies to the importance that this genre assumed, especially in the Biedermeier Era. Pupils seeking to practise this discipline had to draw from nature. Mastery was deemed to consist not only in perfecting the purely technical skills required to fire such large items, but also in achieving refinement in the nuances of colour.

PORCELAIN FACTORY OF KONRAD VON SORGENTHAL

Single coffee set with gold relief decoration on a light blue background,

c. 1798

III.37

VIENNESE PORCELAIN FACTORY

Topograpical Tête-à-Tête, *c.* 1808

III.38

PORCELAIN FACTORY OF KONRAD VON SORGENTHAL
Single tea or coffee set with silhouette portraits, *c.* 1801
III.39

PORCELAIN FACTORY OF KONRAD VON SORGENTHAL
Cup and saucer with a red background, *c.* 1798
Cup and saucer with a light green background, *c.* 1798
III.40

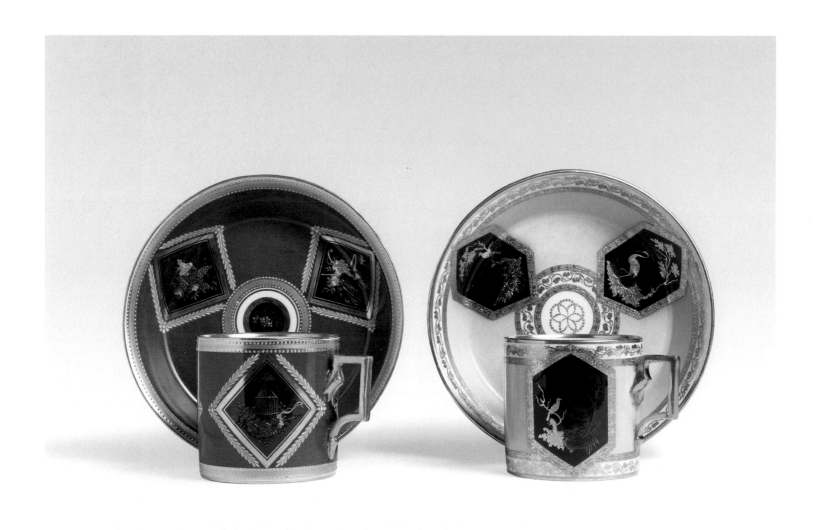

ANONYMOUS VIENNESE MANUFACTURER
Console table with six Doric columns, *c.* 1825
III.42

PETER HUBERT DESVIGNES 1804–83, designer
Console table (III.43) and frame with Portrait
of the Future Prince Johann II von Liechtenstein on a White Pony
by Friedrich von Amerling (III.19), 1840s,
from the Neo-Rococo furnishings of the Liechtenstein
City Palace in Bankgasse, Vienna

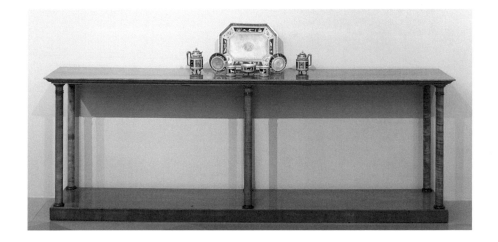

III.1 / p. 118
Josef Rebell (1787–1828)
The Eruption of Vesuvius at Night, 1822
Oil on canvas, 82 x 114 cm
Signed and dated at right: Jos.Rebell 1808.
Inv. no. GE 1384
Provenance: acquired in 1823 from Josef Rebell,
along with the *View of Atrani on the Gulf of Salerno*
(inv. no. GE 1839), by Prince Johann I von Liecht-
enstein

III.2 / pp. 119–20
Josef Rebell (1787–1828)
View of Atrani on the Gulf of Salerno, 1822
Oil on canvas, 81 x 114 cm
Signed and dated at lower right: Jos: Rebell 1822.
Inv. no. GE 1839
Provenance: acquired in 1823 from Josef Rebell,
along with *The Eruption of Vesuvius at Night* (inv.
no. GE 1384), by Prince Johann I von Liechtenstein

III.3 / p. 121
Thomas Ender (1793–1875)
The Gulf of Sorrento
Oil on canvas, 76 x 106 cm
Signed at lower right: Tho.Ender.
Inv. no. GE 2133
Provenance: seized from a Jewish collection in
Austria in 1938; in 1956 in storage in the Charter-
house at Mauerbach; in 1995 presented by the
Austrian Republic, in restitution, to the Jüdische
Kultusgemeinde, Vienna; in 1996 acquired by
Prince Hans-Adam II von und zu Liechtenstein at
auction at Christie's, Mauerbach

III.4 / p. 122
Fedinand Georg Waldmüller (1793–1865)
*The Ruins of the Greek Theatre at Taormina
on Sicily*, 1844
Oil on panel, 38 x 60 cm
Signed and dated at centre of lower edge:
Waldmüller 1844, Inv. no. GE 1595
Provenance: before 1872 at the Galerie Gsell,
Vienna; in the possession of M. J. Kohn; acquired
in 1891 by Prince Johann II von Liechtenstein from
the Viennese art dealer Siegmund Lebel

III.5 / pp. 123–24
Ferdinand Georg Waldmüller (1793–1865)
*The Ruins of the Temple of Juno Lacinia at
Agrigento, c.*1845
Oil on panel, 31 x 39 cm
Signed at lower right: Waldmüller
Inv. no. GE 1599
Provenance: acquired in 1890 by Prince Johann II
von Liechtenstein at the auction house of C. J.
Wawra, Vienna

III.6 / p. 125
Ferdinand Georg Waldmüller (1793–1865)
The Temple of Concord at Agrigento, 1849
Oil on panel, 32 x 40 cm
Signed and dated at centre of lower edge:
Waldmüller 1849
Inv. no. GE 1596
Provenance: before 1872 at the Galerie Gsell,
Vienna, as part of the Caruta Collection; acquired
in 1890 by Prince Johann II von Liechtenstein at
the auction house of C. J. Wawra, Vienna

III.7 / p. 126
Rudolf von Alt (1812–1905)
The Piazza del Duomo in Como
Watercolour over pencil on paper, 18 x 25 cm
Signed at lower right: R Alt
Inv. no. GR 21
Provenance: acquired in 1885 by Prince Joahnn II
von Liechtenstein at the Trenkler auction in Vienna

III.8 / p. 127
Rudolf von Alt (1812–1905)
View of Naples
Watercolour on paper, 30 x 41 cm
Signed at centre of lower edge: R. Alt
Inv. no. GR 316
Provenance: presented by the province of Lower
Austria in 1986, as an 80th-birthday gift to Prince
Franz Josef II von und zu Liechtenstein

III.9 / pp. 128–29
Ferdinand Georg Waldmüller (1793–1865)
*Mountain Landscape with the Ruin of Liechtenstein
near Mödling*, 1859
Oil on panel, 42 x 53 cm
Signed and dated at lower left: Waldmüller 1859.
Inv. no. GE 1603
Provenance: Leistler Collection, Vienna; before
1885 in the collection of Julius Trenkler, Vienna;
acquired in 1891 by Prince Johann II von Liechten-
stein at the auction house of C. J. Wawra, Vienna

III.10 / p. 130
Ferdinand Georg Waldmüller (1793–1865)
View of Mödling, 1848
Oil on canvas, 56 x 69 cm
Signed and dated at lower right: Waldmüller 1848
Inv. no. GE 1604
Provenance: before 1872 at the Galerie Gsell,
Vienna; Etienne R. von Scavani; acquired in 1908
by Prince Johann II von Liechtenstein

III.11 / p. 131
Ferdinand Georg Waldmüller (1793–1865)
*Lime-kiln in the Hinterbrühl, c.*1845
Oil on panel, 44 x 55 cm
Inv. no. GE 1605
Provenance: in 1907 at the art dealer Artaria &
Co., Vienna; acquired in 1912 by Prince Johann II
von Liechtenstein at the auction house of C. J.
Wawra, Vienna

III.12 / p. 132
Ferdinand Georg Waldmüller (1793–1865)
*Lake Fuschl with the Schafberg, c.*1835
Oil on cardboard, 27 x 45 cm
Inv. no. GE 1602
Provenance: acquired in 1913 by Prince Johann II
von Liechtenstein at the auction house of C. J.
Wawra, Vienna

III.13 / p. 133
Thomas Ender (1793–1875)
*The Vogelmaier Ochsenkar Kees in the Rauris
Valley in the High Tauern*, 1834
Oil on canvas, 27 x 36 cm
Signed at lower left: ThoEnder
Inv. no. GE 2001
Provenance: acquired in 1982 by Prince Franz
Josef II von und zu Liechtenstein

III.14 / pp. 134–35
Friedrich Gauermann (1807–62)
The Harvest Wagon, 1837
Oil on canvas, 81 x 97 cm
Signed and dated at lower left: F. Gauermann. /
f. 1837.
Inv. no. GE 2103
Provenance: acquired in 1838 from Friedrich
Gauermann by F. A. Fleischhacker; Ignatz Bieder-
mann; acquired in 1902 by Prince Johann II von
Liechtenstein

III.15 / p. 136
Friedrich von Amerling (1803–87)
*Portrait of Princess Marie Franziska von Liechten-
stein (1834–1909) at the Age of Two*, 1836
Oil on cardboard, 33 x 27 cm
Signed and dated at lower right: Fr. Amerling 1836
Inv. no. GE 2314
Provenance: acquired in 1927 by Prince Johann II
von Liechtenstein from his sister Princess Therese
Maria of Bavaria

III.16 / pp. 137–38
Friedrich von Amerling (1803–87)
*Portrait of Princess Karoline von Liechtenstein
(1836–85) at the Age of One and a Half*, 1837
Oil on canvas, 35 x 28 cm
Inv. no. GE 2315
Provenance: acquired in 1927 by Prince Johann II
von Liechtenstein from his sister Therese Maria of
Bavaria

III.17 / p. 139
Friedrich von Amerling (1803–87)
*Portrait of Princess Sophie von Liechtenstein
(1837–99) at the Age of about One and a Half*,
1838
Oil on canvas, 34 x 28 cm
Inv. no. GE 2379
Provenance: acquired in 1927 by Prince Johann II
von Liechtenstein from his sister Therese Maria
of Bavaria

III.18 / p. 140
Friedrich von Amerling (1803–87)
Oil sketch for the *Portrait of the Future Prince
Johann II von Liechtenstein (1840–1929) on a
White Pony*, 1844/45
Oil on canvas, 33 x 24 cm
Inv. no. GE 2106
Provenance: in 1888 listed in the inventory of
Amerling's estate; acquired by Prince Johann II
von Liechtenstein from the Viennese hotel owner
Johann Frohmer

III.19 / p. 141
Friedrich von Amerling (1803–87)
*Portrait of the Future Prince Johann II von Liechten-
stein (1840–1929) on a White Pony*, 1845
Oil on canvas, 234 x 157 cm
In the original Neo-Rococo frame forming part of
the decoration of the City Palace in Bankgasse,
Vienna, 1843–47
Signed and dated at lower right: Fr. Amerling 1845
Inv. no. GE 2381
Provenance: commissioned in 1845 by Prince
Alois II von Liechtenstein

III.20 / p. 142
Unknown artist in the circle of Heinrich von Füger
(1751–1818)
*Portrait of the Children of Prince Johann I von
Liechtenstein: Princess Ida Leopoldine
(1811–84) and Prince Rudolf (1816–48)*,
c. 1820
Oil on canvas, 105 x 108 cm
Inv. no. GE 1979, companion piece to inv. no.
GE 1972
Provenance: commissioned, along with three
further double portraits of children, by Prince
Johann I von Liechtenstein; until 1944 in the
'Family Room' at the manor house at Eisgrub

III.21 / p. 143
Unknown artist in the circle of Heinrich von Füger
(1751–18)
*Portrait of the Sons of Prince Johann I von Liech-
tenstein: Prince Franz de Paula (1802–87) and
Prince Karl Johann (1803–71)*, c. 1815
Oil on canvas, 103 x 104 cm
Inv. no. GE 1972, companion piece to inv. no.
GE 1979
Provenance: commissioned, along with three
further double portraits of children, by Prince
Johann I von Liechtenstein; until 1944 in the
'Family Room' at the manor house at Eisgrub

III.22 / pp. 144–45
Fedinand Georg Waldmüller (1793–1865)
*Portrait of the Future Emperor Franz Josef I
of Austria (1830–1916) as a Grenadier with
Toy Soldiers*, 1832
Oil on panel, 35 x 29 cm
Signed and dated at lower left on the drum:
Waldmüller 1832
Inv. no. GE 1606
Provenance: before 1913 in the possession of
Archduke Rainer in Hernstein; before 1931 in the
possession of Leopold Salvator Habsburg-Lothring-
en; before 1975 in the possession of Franz
Josef Habsburg-Lothringen in Berndorf; until 2002
in a private collection in Vienna; acquired by
Prince Hans-Adam II von und zu Liechtenstein
at the Wiener Kunstauktionen

III.23 / p. 147
Ferdinand Georg Waldmüller (1793–1865)
Portrait of Thiery, Landlord of the Wolf-in-the-Meadow Inn, 1833
Oil on canvas, 66 x 53 cm
Signed and dated at upper right: Waldmüller 1833.
Inv. no. GE 1608
Provenance: private collection in Vienna; private collection in Munich; acquired in 2003 by Prince Hans-Adam II von und zu Liechtenstein

III.24 / p. 148
Ferdinand Georg Waldmüller (1793–1865)
Portrait of the Architect Charles de Moreau (1758–1841), 1822
Oil on canvas, 55 x 45 cm
Signed and dated at lower left: Waldmüller 1822
Inv. no. GE 1597
Provenance: before 1913 in the possession of Klara Schuster, Vienna; Marie Hirnczicz, Vienna; acquired by Prince Johann II von Liechtenstein

III.25 / p. 149
Friedrich von Amerling (1803–87)
Portrait of the Painter Peter Fendi (1796–1842), 1833
Oil on canvas, 52 x 42 cm
Dated at lower left: 10/833
Inv. no. GE 2063

III.26 / p. 150
Friedrich von Amerling (1803–87)
Study of the Head of a Bearded Man
Oil on canvas, 65 x 53 cm
Inv. no. GE 2378

III.27 / p. 151
Friedrich von Amerling (1803–87)
Self-portrait, 1844
Oil on canvas, 53 x 42 cm
Signed and dated at right: F. Amerling 844
Inv. no. GE 2100
Provenance: acquired in 1914 by Prince Johann II von Liechtenstein at the Dorotheum, Vienna

III.28 / p. 152
Franz Eybl (1806–80)
Portrait of the Surgeon Josef Walz
Oil on canvas, 63 x 50 cm
Signed at right: F Eybl
Inv. no. GE 2091
Provenance: acquired in 1913 by Prince Johann II von Liechtenstein at the auction house of C. J. Wawra, Vienna

III.29 / pp. 153–54
Franz Eybl (1806–80)
Berry Picker before a Mountain, 1844
Oil on panel, 42 x 34 cm
Signed and dated at lower right: F. EIBL. 1844.
Inv. no. GE 2092
Provenance: acquired in 1896 by Prince Johann II von Liechtenstein

III.30 / pp. 156–57
Friedrich von Amerling (1803–87)
Lost in her Dreams, c. 1835
Oil on canvas, 55 x 45 cm
Inv. no. GE 1125
Provenance: acquired in 2003 by Prince Hans-Adam II von und zu Liechtenstein at auction at Sotheby's, London

III.31 / p. 155
Friedrich von Amerling (1803–87)
Portrait of Elise Kreuzberger, 1837
Oil on canvas, 57 x 45 cm
Signed and dated at upper left: Fr. Amerling 1837
Inv. no. GE 2377
Provenance: acquired in 1837 by Prince Alois II von Liechtenstein through the mediation of Princess Franziska von Liechtenstein

II.32 / pp. 158–59
Francesco Hayez (1791–1882)
Vengeance is Sworn, 1852
Oil on canvas, 237 x 178 cm
Signed and dated: Fran. Hayez / in Venezia 1851
Inv. no. GE 1642
Provenance: in 1851 in the collection of Enrico Taccioli, Milan; Duke Litta Modignani, Milan; in 1934 in a private collection in Switzerland; acquired in 2003 by Prince Hans-Adam II von und zu Liechtenstein on the Swiss art market

III.33 / p. 160
Franz von Lenbach (1836–1904)
Portrait of the Architect Gottfried Semper (1803–1879)
Oil on canvas, 63 x 50 cm
Signed at lower right: Lenbach
Inv. no. GE 2011
Provenance: acquired in 1909 by Prince Johann II von Liechtenstein from Hans Semper, son of the subject

III.34 / p. 161
Franz von Lenbach (1836–1904)
Portrait of Prince Rudolf von Liechtenstein (1833–1888), 1886
Oil on canvas, 61 x 49 cm
Signed and dated at upper right: Lenbach 1886.
Inv. no. GE 2007
Provenance: acquired in 1920 by Prince Johann II von Liechtenstein

III.35 / p. 162
Joseph Nigg (1782–1863)
Floral Still Life with White Grapes, 1838
Painting on old Viennese porcelain, 69 x 52 cm
Signed and dated at lower left: Jos. Nigg in Wien 1838
Inv. no. PO 2079, companion piece to inv. no. PO 2080
Provenance: acquired in 2004, along with the *Floral Still Life with Black Grapes* (GE 2080), by Prince Hans-Adam II von und zu Liechtenstein on the Viennese art market

Ill.36 / p. 163
Joseph Nigg (1782–1863)
Floral Still Life with Black Grapes, 1838
Painting on old Viennese porcelain, 69 x 52 cm
Signed and dated at lower left: Jos. Nigg 1838
Inv. no. PO 2080, companion piece to inv. no.
PO 2079
Provenance: acquired in 2004, along with the
Floral Still Life with White Grapes (GE 2079), by
Prince Hans-Adam II von und zu Liechtenstein
on the Viennese art market

Ill.37 / p. 165
Porcelain factory of Konrad von Sorgenthal
Single coffee set with gold relief decoration on
a light blue backgroud, *c.* 1798
Tray, coffee pot with lid, milk jug with lid, sugar
bowl with lid, cup and saucer
Painted porcelain, tray: height 31 cm, coffee pot:
height 14 cm, milk jug: height 12 cm, sugar bowl:
height 8 cm, cup: height 6 cm, saucer: diameter
14 cm
Inscription on the base of each item: within a band
in under-glaze blue: various thrower numbers in
white, embosser initial U, engraved stamp for
years 94, 97, and 98
Inv. no. PO 2044
Provenance: collection of Ferdinand Bloch-Bauer,
Vienna; seized in 1940 for the collection of the
Kunstgewerbemuseum, Vienna; restituted to the
heirs of Ferdinand Bloch-Bauer in 2003; acquired
by Prince Hans-Adam von und zu Liechtenstein

Ill.38 / p. 166
Viennese porcelain factory
Topograpical Tête-à-Tête, *c.* 1808
Tray, coffee pot with lid, milk jug with lid, sugar
bowl, two cups and saucer, in their original box
Painted porcelain, tray: width 42 cm, coffee pot:
height 20 cm, milk jug: height 18 cm, sugar
bowl: height 13 cm, cups: height 9 cm, saucers:
diameter 14 cm
Inscription on the base of each piece: within a
band in under-glaze blue: various thrower and
painter numbers in white, engraved stamp for
the years 1807 and 1808

Inscription on the base: Vue de la Ville de Vienne,
de ses Fauxbourgs, et de ses Environs, prise du
Château de Belvedere
Inv. no. PO 2064
Provenance: acquired in 2003 by Prince Hans-
Adam II von und zu Liechtenstein

Ill.39 / p. 167
Porcelain factory of Konrad von Sorgenthal
Single tea or coffee set with silhouette portraits,
c. 1801
Oval tray, large jug with lid, small jug with lid,
cup and saucer
Painted porcelain, tray: width 32 cm, large jug:
height 13 cm, small jug: height 10 cm, sugar
bowl: height 8 cm
Inscription on the base of each piece: within a
band in under-glaze blue: various thrower numbers
in white, embosser initial P, engraved stamp for
the years 1800 and 1801
Inv. no. PO 2072
Provenance: acquired in 2003 by Prince Hans-
Adam II von und zu Liechtenstein

Ill.40 / p. 168
Porcelain factory of Konrad von Sorgenthal
Cup and saucer with a red background, *c.* 1798
Cup and saucer with a light green background,
c. 1798
Painted porcelain, cups: height 6 cm, saucers:
diameter 13 cm
Inscription on the base of each piece: within a
band in under-glaze blue: various thrower and
painter numbers in white, engraved stamp for
the year 98
Inv. no. PO 2046
Provenance: collection of Ferdinand Bloch-Bauer,
Vienna; seized in 1940 for the collection of the
Kunstgewerbemuseum, Vienna; acquired in 2003
by Prince Hans-Adam II von und zu Liechtenstein

Ill.41 / p. 169
Viennese porcelain factory
Cup (with view of the Bach Circus) and saucer,
c. 1811
Painted porcelain, cup: height 6 cm, saucer:
diameter 14 cm
Inscription on the base of each piece: within a
band in under-glaze blue, various thrower numbers
in white, painter number 155 (Joseph Kürner) in
gold, engraved stamp for the year 1811
Inscription on the base of the cup: Vue Cercle
gymnastique au Prater.
Inv. no. PO 2081
Provenance: acquired in 2004 by Prince Hans-
Adam II von und zu Liechtenstein from a private
collection through Alexander Rudiger, London

Ill.42 / p. 170
Anonymous Viennese manufacturer
Console table with six Doric columns, *c.* 1825
Acorn veneer over a soft-wood core, height 86
cm, width 253 cm, depth 54 cm
Inv. no. MO 1577

Ill.43 / p. 171
Peter Hubert Desvignes (1804–83), design
Console table, 1840s
From the Neo-Rococo furnishings of the Liechten-
stein City Palace in Bankgasse, Vienna
Wood, mirror glass, Carrara marble (table top),
height 86 cm, width 181 cm, depth 69 cm
Inv. no. MO 1568
Provenance: decoration of the Liechtenstein
City Palace in Bankgasse, Vienna

APPENDIX

INDEX OF NAMES

THE HOLDINGS OF THE PRINCELY COLLECTIONS

Exh. cat. *Wiener Biedermeier-Malerei und Carl Spitzweg. Aus den Sammlungen des Fürsten von Liechtenstein*, by Gustav Wilhelm, Kunstmuseum Luzern, Lucerne 1950.

Exh. cat. *Deutsche Malerei 15.–19. Jahrhundert aus den Sammlungen des Regierenden Fürsten von Liechtenstein*, by Reinhold Baumstark, Staatliche Kunstsammlung Vaduz, Vaduz 1979.

Exh. cat. *Wiener Biedermeier. Gemälde aus den Sammlungen des Regierenden Fürsten von Liechtenstein*, by Reinhold Baumstark, Staatliche Kunstsammlung Vaduz, Vaduz 1979.

Baumstark, Reinhold: *Meisterwerke der Sammlungen des Fürsten von Liechtenstein. Gemälde*, Zurich/Munich 1980.

Exh. cat. *Liechtenstein – The Princely Collections*, issued by the Metropolitan Museum of Art, Washington, DC/Sammlungen des Fürsten von Liechtenstein, Vaduz (with contributions by Reinhold Baumstark, James D. Draper, Georg Kugler, Sir John Pope-Hennessy, Olga Raggio, Dominique Thiébaut etc.), Metropolitan Museum of Art, New York 1985.

Die Sammlungen des Fürsten von Liechtenstein (with contributions by Walter Koschatzky, Johann Kräftner, Manfred Leithe-Jasper, Hellmut Lorenz, Evelin Oberhammer, Wolfgang Prohaska, Karl Schütz, Uwe Wieczorek, Christian Witt-Doerring), special issue of *Parnass*, vol. 15 (1995), no. 11.

HOUSE OF LIECHTENSTEIN

Wolf, Adam: *Fürstin Eleonore Liechtenstein. 1745–1812. Nach Briefen und Memoiren ihrer Zeit*, Vienna 1875.

Falke, Jacob: *Geschichte des fürstlichen Hauses Liechtenstein*, 3 vols., Vienna 1868/1877/1882.

Criste, Oskar: *Feldmarschall Johannes Fürst von Liechtenstein. Eine Biographie*, Vienna 1905.

Stekl, Hannes: *Österreichs Aristokratie im Vormärz. Herrschaftsstil und Lebensformen der Fürstenhäuser Liechtenstein und Schwarzenberg*, Vienna 1973 (Sozial- und wirtschaftshistorische Studien).

Wilhelm, Gustav: *Die Fürsten von Liechtenstein und ihre Beziehungen zu Kunst und Wissenschaft*, Schaan 1976 (Sonderdruck aus dem Jahrbuch der Liechtensteinischen Kunstgesellschaft).

NEOCLASSICISM AND BIEDERMEIER

Exh. cat. *Romantik und Realismus in Österreich. Gemälde und Zeichnungen aus der Sammlung Georg Schäfer Schweinfurt*, by Konrad Kaiser, Schloss Laxenburg, Munich 1968.

Koschatzky, Walter: *Österreichische Aquarellmalerei 1750–1900*, Freiburg/Vienna 1987.

Exh. cat. *Bürgersinn und Aufbegehren. Biedermeier und Vormärz in Wien 1815–1848*, Historisches Museum der Stadt Wien, Vienna 1987.

Haskell, Francis/ Penny, Nicholas: *Taste and the Antique. The Lure of Classical Sculpture, 1500–1900*, New Haven, CT/ London 1988.

Exh. cat. *Wiener Biedermeier. Malerei zwischen Wiener Kongress und Revolution*, ed. Gerbert Frodl and Klaus Albrecht Schröder, Kunstforum der Bank Austria Wien und Österreichische Galerie Wien, Munich 1992.

Frodl, Gerbert: *Wiener Malerei der Biedermeierzeit*, Rosenheim 1997.

Sturm-Bednarczyk, Elisabeth/Jobst, Claudia: *Wiener Porzellan des Klassizismus. Die Ära Conrad von Sorgenthal 1784–1805*, Vienna 2000.

Exh. cat. *Dall'Accademia all'Atelier. Pittori tra Brera e il Canton Ticino nell'Ottocento*, ed. Maria Angela Previtera and Sergio Rebora, Pinacoteca Cantonale Giovanni Züst, Milan 2000.

Exh. cat. *Italienische Reisen. Landschaftsbilder österreichischer und ungarischer Maler. 1770–1850*, ed. Sabine Grabner and Claudia Wöhrer, Österreichische Galerie Belvedere Wien, Vienna 2001.

Frodl, Gerbert (ed.): *Geschichte der bildenden Kunst in Österreich*, vol. 5, Munich/Berlin/London/New York and Vienna 2002.

Exh. cat. *Antike in Wien. Die Akademie und der Klassizismus um 1800*, by Bettina Hagen, Akademie der Bildenden Künste Wien-Gemäldegalerie, Mainz 2002.

ARCHITECTURE AND LANDSCAPE ARCHITECTURE

Rizzi, W. Georg: 'Joseph Kornhäusels Wiener Bauten für den Fürsten Liechtenstein'; in: *Alte und moderne Kunst*, vol. 22 (1977), no. 152, pp. 23–29.

Schwarz, Mario: 'Klassizismus und Romantik auf den Besitzungen des Fürsten Liechtenstein'; in: Schwarz, Mario: *Architektur des Klassizismus und der Romantik in Niederösterreich*, St Pölten/

Vienna 1982 (Wissenschaftliche Schriftenreihe Niederösterreich 62/63), pp. 39–44.

Kräftner, Johann: 'Am Ozean der Stille. Der Landschaftsgarten zwischen Feldsberg und Eisgrub in Südmähren'; in: *Parnass*, vol. 7 (1987), no. 4, pp. 33–43.

Kräftner, Johann: 'Joseph Kornhäusel. Der vergessene Biedermeierarchitekt'; in: *Parnass*, vol. 7 (1987), no. 3, pp. 49–67.

Kräftner, Johann: 'Joseph Kornhäusel. Un Architecte oublie de l'Epoque Biedermeier'; in: *Archives d'Architecture Moderne*, vol. 1988, no. 37, pp. 16–67.

Wilhelm, Gustav: *Joseph Hardtmuth. Architekt und Erfinder. 1758–1816*, Vienna/Cologne 1990.

PAINTING AND SCULPTURE

Burg, Hermann: *Der Bildhauer Franz Anton Zauner und seine Zeit. Ein Beitrag zur Geschichte des Klassizismus in Österreich*, Vienna 1915.

Poch-Kalous, Margarethe: *Johann Martin Fischer*, Vienna 1949 (Forschungen zur Österreichischen Kunstgeschichte, vol. 3).

Exh. cat. *Angelika Kaufmann und ihre Zeitgenossen*, Vorarlberger Landesmuseum Bregenz and Österreichisches Museum für Angewandte Kunst Wien, Vienna 1968/69.

Krasa-Florian, Selma: *Johann Nepomuk Schaller 1777–1842. Ein Wiener Bildhauer aus dem Freundeskreis der Nazarener*, Vienna 1977.

Praz, Mario/ Pavanello, *Giuseppe: L'opera completa del Canova*, Milan 1976.

Koschatzky, Walter: *Thomas Ender. 1793–1875. Kammermaler Erzherzog Johanns*, Graz 1982.

Exh. cat. *Rudolf von Alt 1812–1905. Die schönsten Aquarelle aus den acht Jahrzehnten seines Schaffens*, Graphische Sammlung Albertina Wien, Vienna 1984.

Licht, Fred: *Antonio Canova. Beginn der modernen Skulptur*, Munich 1983.

Arisi, Ferdinando: *Gian Paolo Panini e i fasti della Roma del'700*, Rome 1986.

Feuchtmüller, Rupert: *Friedrich Gauermann. 1807–1862*, Rosenheim 1987.

Exh. cat. *Ferdinand Georg Waldmüller*, ed. Klaus Albrecht Schröder, Kunstforum Länderbank Wien, Munich 1990.

Exh. cat. *Antonio Canova*, Museo Correr Venice/ Gipsoteca Possagno, Venice 1992.

Exh. cat. *Giovanni Paolo Panini. 1691–1765*, ed. Ferdinando Arisi, Palazzo Gotico Piacenza, Milan 1993.

Feuchtmüller, Rupert: *Ferdinand Georg Waldmüller. 1793–1865. Leben – Schriften – Werke*, Vienna/ Munich 1996.

Schemper-Sparholz, Ingeborg: '"Le Désir d'Avoir la Nature en Marbre". Die Sitzstatue der Prinzessin Leopoldine Esterházy-Liechtenstein von Antonio Canova und das Frauenbild der Frühromantik'; issued by: Bundesdenkmalamt Wien/ Institut für Kunstgeschichte der Universität Wien: *Wiener Jahrbuch für Kunstgeschichte*, vol. L, special issue, Vienna/Cologne/Weimar 1997.

Exh. cat. *Angelika Kauffmann*, ed. Bettina Baumgärtel, Kunstmuseum Düsseldorf, Düsseldorf 1998.

Koschatzky, Walter: *Rudolf von Alt*, Vienna/ Cologne/Weimar 2001.

Krug, Wolfgang: *Friedrich Gauermann. 1807–1862. Aus der Sammlung des Niederösterreichischen Landesmuseums*, Vienna/ Munich 2001.

Exh. cat. *Un ritrattista nell'Europa delle corti. Giovanni Battista Lampi. 1751–1830*, by Ferdinando Mazzocca, Roberto Pancheri etc., Castello del Buonconsilio, Trent 2001.

Prost, Franz (ed.): *'Der Natur und Kunst gewidmet'. Der Esterházysche Schlosspark in Eisenstadt*, Vienna/Cologne/Weimar 2001.

Exh. cat. *Friedrich von Amerling. 1803–1887*, ed. Sabine Grabner, Österreichische Galerie Belvedere Wien, Vienna/Leipzig 2003.

FRIEDRICH VON AMERLING
Vienna 1803–Vienna 1887
Waldmüller (qv) and Amerling were the most highly regarded Austrian portrait painters of the nineteenth century. After attending the Academy of Fine Arts in Vienna, Amerling studied painting in both London (where he was taught by Thomas Lawrence) and Paris (where he studied under Horace Vernet). On returning to Vienna, he rapidly became established as a portrait painter. Especially from the mid-1820s to the revolutionary year of 1848, Amerling's portraits were much in demand among the Austrian nobility, above all the ruling House of Habsburg. His outstanding gift for observation resulted not only in pure 'studies of character', but was also applied to recording his sitters' sense of their own status as members of the aristocracy or the bourgeoisie. In Amerling's paintings we find a dazzling reflection of Austrian society of the late Biedermeier Era. Especially striking are Amerling's portraits of the family, and in particular the children, of Alois II von Liechtenstein. Together with other works by Amerling, these are preserved in the Princely Collections.

BERNARDO BELLOTTO
Venice 1721–Venice 1780
Like Antonio Canale, called Canaletto, and Francesco Guardi, Bellotto was one of the most celebrated exponents of the painting of Venetian views, or vedute. He was the nephew and pupil of Canaletto, and shared this nickname. While Canaletto and Guardi remained in their native city, Bellotto left Venice for good in 1747. His pictures, most of which show almost panoramic views of cities, are notable for their minute detail. These vedute were intended as authentic documents of the properties and residences of the various rulers who appointed Bellotto as court painter. In 1758–59 Bellotto spent two years in Vienna. During his stay there he produced thirteen pictures for Empress Maria Theresia, one for her chancellor Count Kaunitz, and two of the Garden Palace at Rossau for Prince Joseph Wenzel von Liechtenstein. These last are still to be found in the Princely Collections.

ANTONIO CANOVA
Possagno, near Treviso 1757–Venice 1822
Canova is regarded as the most innovative sculptor of Neoclassicism. In many respects his work appears to give form to the ideals upheld by the renowned eighteenth-century German art historian Johann Joachim Winckelmann. For his early masterpiece Daedalus and Icarus (1778/79, Venice, Museo Correr), Canova still mediated between a traditional form of naturalism and the emerging current of Neoclassicism. In 1779 Canova went to Rome and there evolved his revolutionary new style, which linked an unprecedented rigour and simplicity with an idealised beauty. His tomb of Pope Clement XIV (1783/87, Rome, SS. Apostoli) provided the first clear evidence of this stylistic shift. Canova then went on to devise an altogether new type of monumental tomb, for Titian, the celebrated Renaissance painter, and this was adapted for his Tomb of Marie Christine of Austria (1798–1805, Vienna, Augustinerkirche). In his commitment to the Italian Purismo movement, Canova went far beyond the idealising formal canon of Classical Antiquity. He was especially acclaimed for his Amor and Psyche (1783–93, Paris, Musée du Louvre) and his Three Graces (1812/16, St Petersburg, Hermitage). The most fascinating of his portraits, in which he often combined a classical format with the naturalistic rendering of individual character, is Pauline Borghese as Venus (1804/08, Rome, Galleria Borghese).

PETER HUBERT DESVIGNES
Constantinople 1804–Hither Green, Kent (now Lewisham, Greater London) 1883
Desvignes initially studied under William Atkinson at the Royal Academy in London. In 1835 he took part in a competition to design a new building for the British Houses of Parliament. Here, for the first time, he was confronted with a project that required the architect to evolve a new system of communication for a multi-partite organism not only partly within an existing architectural structure but also taking this last into account. When he received the commission to redesign the Liechtenstein

palace in Vienna in the Neo-Rococo style, a task that occupied him from at least 1837 until around 1849, he addressed a similar challenge. His redesign marks not only the highpoint of his otherwise obscure career, but is also one of the most elaborate and ambitious design projects to be implemented in the nineteenth century. Although he later returned to England, Desvignes had difficulty regaining a foothold there, and very little is known of the last decades of his life.

THOMAS ENDER
Vienna 1793–Vienna 1875
Like his twin brother, Johann Nepomuk Ender, Thomas Ender initially studied at the Viennese Academy of Fine Arts. Here, with Josef Mössmer and Franz Steinfeld as his teachers and the seventeenth-century painters Claude Lorrain and Jacob van Ruisdael as his models, he specialised in landscape painting. In 1813 he joined a Natural History expedition to Brazil, as the team's painter. Thanks to a stipend granted by Prince Metternich, he was able to spend four years in Rome (1819–22). He later accompanied Archduke Johann of Austria on numerous journeys through the Habsburg domains, but also to the south of Russia and the Far East. In the 1850s he again travelled to Italy, spending time in Rome and Naples. Well over a thousand drawings and watercolours survive as a record of this intensive commitment to travel. Ender's appointments to a Professorship at the Viennese Academy and to a place on the Imperial Advisory Council were themselves a testament to the high regard for his work as a painter.

FRANZ EYBL
Vienna 1806–Vienna 1880

Eybl trained under Josef Mössmer in the Department of Landscape at the Viennese Academy of Fine Arts, where he also took up the new technique of lithography. He took further classes in History Painting under Lampi (qv) and Franz Caucig. Of greater significance, however, was his encounter with the large and imposing compositions of the Austrian history painter Krafft (qv). In the 1860s Eybl was equalled only by Josef Kriehuber as a portrait painter and portrait lithographer to the Viennese nobility and bourgeoisie. From the 1830s he had devoted himself above all to genre painting, treating subjects largely drawn from the Salzkammergut. Until 1848 he was widely regarded as the chief master of this type of painting. In 1843 Eybl was elected a member of the Viennese Academy, and in 1853 he was appointed Curator of the Imperial Picture Gallery. In his last years his productivity as a painter decreased on account of his involvement in picture restoration.

JOHANN MARTIN FISCHER
Bebele, near Füssen 1740–Vienna 1820

Fischer arrived in Vienna in 1760 in order to train with the sculptor Anton Tabota. In 1762–66 he studied under Jakob Schletterer at the Viennese Academy of Fine Arts. In 1785 he was elected a member of the Academy and was subsequently appointed to the Professorships of Sculpture (as successor to Zauner, qv) and of Anatomy. He owed this last post to the celebrated teacher of Ophthalmology and Anatomy at the University of Vienna, Joseph Barth, a lifelong friend. Barth was not only one of the most celebrated physicians of his age, but also a great collector and munificent patron of the arts. Fischer's appointment as Director of the Viennese Academy in 1815 marked the highpoint of his academic career. He received sculptural commissions above all from public institutions and persons of high social standing. He provided sculptural works, including fountains, for many city squares and other public places in Vienna. One of his most important patrons was the House of Liechtenstein. He was commissioned to redesign the Liechtenstein palace in Herrengasse, Vienna; and, for the park of the manor house at Eisgrub, he made a large sculptural group, the *Three Graces*.

MARCANTONIO FRANCESCHINI
Bologna 1648–Bologna 1729

Franceschini trained in the tradition of Bolognese Neoclassicism under Carlo Cignani, himself a pupil of Francesco Albani. By comparison with his Italian painter colleagues, however, Franceschini applied the principles of this style with particular rigour and consistency and, in this respect, his work may be said to be closer to the French Neoclassicism of an artist such as Eustache Le Sueur. Franceschini produced large altarpieces as well as exquisite easel paintings; but his particular gift was for extensive fresco cycles, and these account for much of his output. Prince Johann Adam Andreas I von Liechtenstein, who commissioned the building of a Garden Palace, had a particular liking for Franceschini. From 1692 until his death, the artist conducted a lively correspondence with this patron, much of which survives, providing a unique cultural-historical document of their relationship. Franceschini was responsible for a great many of the paintings on canvas originally intended for the ceilings and walls of the Garden Palace.

HEINRICH VON FÜGER
Heilbronn 1751–Vienna 1818

After studying law in Halle, Füger trained as an artist in Leipzig under Adam Friedrich Oeser and, during this time, resolved once and for all to embark on an artistic career. In 1774 he travelled south, via Dresden, to Vienna, where he was soon receiving commissions from the Imperial Court. He initially specialised in the painting of miniatures, in particular portrait miniatures, but later favoured portraits on a large scale. From 1776 he sojourned at length in Rome and Naples, where he devoted himself to the study of the art of Antiquity and of the Renaissance. While in Italy he came to know the painters Anton Raffael Mengs and Jacques-Louis David, both of whom exerted a strong influence on the stylistic development of his work. In 1783 he returned to Vienna. Here, in 1795, he was appointed Director of the Academy of Fine Arts, where the greater part of his surviving oeuvre is to be found. Füger ended his career as Director of the Imperial Picture Gallery, a position he held from 1806. He made his reputation as a history painter and was a pioneer of Neoclassicism in Austria.

FRIEDRICH GAUERMANN
Miesenbach 1807–Vienna 1862

The work of the landscape and animal painter Gauermann is closely connected with rural life in the Austrian Alps. In his paintings he succeeded in blending landscape with both human and animal figures, these combinations being presented in both atmospheric scenes and dramatic episodes. His approach to rendering the natural world followed less in the tradition of his father, and first teacher, the landscape painter Jakob Gauermann, than in that in which he was trained in 1824–27 at the Viennese Academy of Fine Arts. Of even more influence on his own style, however, was the example of Dutch painting of the seventeenth century, which Gauermann studied through making numerous copies. Gauermann's work was enthusiastically received by his contemporaries and was soon much in demand. His paintings were also much admired by the House of Liechtenstein; as a guest at the hunting parties on the Liechtenstein estates in Moravia, he was able to make preparatory sketches for his animal paintings. Seven sketchbooks, numerous drawings, and seventeen paintings in the Princely Collections testify to the high regard of several generations of the family for this artist.

MARTEN JOZEF GEERAERTS
(Christened in) Antwerp 1707–Antwerp 1791
Geeraerts's speciality was the painted imitation of
friezes or reliefs in stone or wood, a much-loved
form of decoration in the seventeenth and eighteenth centuries. For the former Abbey of St Peter
in Ghent, he provided a cycle of nine pictures with
the emblems of the Arts and Sciences, which were
matched to motifs carved in the wooden panels
into which they were set. In the Princely Collections
there are three scenes with putti, signed and dated
1752, made in imitation of stone relief.

GIOVANNI GHISOLFI
Milan 1623–Milan 1683
In 1650 Ghisolfi travelled to Rome, where he
worked for a while in the studio of Salvator Rosa.
Influenced, above all, by the Classical compositions
of Pietro da Cortona, he evolved a picture type of
his own in the 1660s: this combined landscape
with architectural fragments and the ruins of Antiquity and was later much in demand. Ghisolfi was
also active as a fresco painter: in 1664 he decorated the Palazzo Trissino Baston and the Palazzo
Giustiniani Baggio with extensive series of landscape frescoes, which have only partly been preserved. In collaboration with Antonio Busca, he
worked on the decorative frescoes in the gallery of
the Palazzo Borromeo Arese in Cesano Maderno,
near Milan; and in 1680 he worked with Federico
Bianchi at the Villa Litta Modigliani in Varese. Today
Ghisolfi is best known for his capriccios, his small
landscapes with ruins worked up into sentimental
scenes enlivened through the addition of figures. In
this role, he may be regarded as the precursor of
Pannini (qv).

JOSEPH HARDTMUTH
Aspern an der Zaya 1758–Vienna 1816
Joseph Hardtmuth embarked on his artistic career
in the studio of Joseph Meissl, who from 1787 had
served as court architect to Prince Franz Josef I
von Liechtenstein. Hardtmuth inherited his
teacher's post after the latter's death in 1790. His
first important project for the House of Liechtenstein was commissioned in 1792 by Prince Alois I:
the Liechtenstein Palace in Herrengasse. To begin
with, Hardtmuth was asked to design its façade,
and he then assumed responsibility for the project
as a whole, including the decoration of the library
and the living quarters, and the preparation of the
stables and the riding school. Thereafter, he was
commissioned to oversee all architectural projects
on the Liechtenstein estates. In the park at Eisgrub
he erected a Temple to the Sun and a Turkish
Tower, and he conceived the Hansenburg, in imitation of a medieval castle. His Memorial Temple,
erected in the Vorderbrühl in the Vienna Woods in
1811 to mark the victory over Napoleon at the
Battle of Aspern, collapsed the very next year. Its
reconstruction was undertaken by Joseph Kornhäusel. Kornhäusel also built the Temple of Diana
near Feldsberg after Hardtmuth's plans because
the latter had, in 1812, sought to end his contract
with the Prince. His post then passed to Kornhäusel. Hardtmuth is also remembered as the
inventor of various technical processes, such as
those used in the manufacture of so-called Viennese earthenware and of Austrian lead pencils.

FRANCESCO HAYEZ
Venice 1791–Milan 1882
Hayez is regarded as the most important Italian
representative of History Painting in the Era of
Romanticism. He was strongly marked by his train-
ing at the Venetian Academy, which had been mod-
ernised by Count Leopoldo Cicognara, and under
the Neoclassicist Teodoro Mateini. From 1809 in
Rome he made an intensive study of the work of
Raphael and came to know the sculptor Antonio
Canova (qv), who was to exert a great influence on
his subsequent work. The masterpiece of his Neo-

classical phase was *Rinaldo and Armida* (Venice,
Ca' Pesaro). His painting Pietro Rossi (Turin, private
collection), with its new style and its medieval subject, became an effective manifesto for the emerging current of Romanticism in painting. Hayez
moved to Milan on being appointed to a Professorship at the Brera Academy. Here, he painted historical role portraits of outstanding personalities in
public life. As a history painter he evinced a particular interest in Italian themes. In one of his most
enthusiastically received paintings, *The Thirst of
the Crusaders at the Walls of Jerusalem* (1838,
Turin, Palazzo Reale), there are traces of the influence of both seventeenth-century Venetian and
nineteenth-century German painting. These sources
were to be of particular significance for his later
output. After the upheavals of 1848, in which
Hayez took part, he again turned to allegorical
scenes with a political background.

MAERTEN VAN HEEMSKERCK
Heemskerck 1498–Haarlem 1574
Maerten van Heemskerck was inspired to travel
south by his older painter-colleague Jan van Scorel,
who in 1524 had returned to Haarlem from his own
visit to Italy. During his stay in Italy, from 1532 to
1537, Heemskerck made an intensive study of the
work of Michelangelo, Raphael, and Giulio Romano,
whose influence he later ensured in the Nether-
lands. His own rather grandiose style of painting,
with its emphasis on human anatomy, testifies also
to his interest in the sculpture of Roman Antiquity.
Heemskerck made numerous drawn records of the
newly excavated ruins of Ancient Rome. These later
served as the starting point for fantastical painted
compositions. In addition to altarpieces, portraits,
and history paintings on religious and mythological
themes, he produced a large number of drawings
for the print trade. By means of this form of repro-
duction, Heemskerck's compositions served to dis-
seminate a Mannerist style in northern Europe.

ANTON HICKEL
Böhmisch-Leipa (now Česká Lipa, Czech Republic) 1745–Hamburg 1798

Hickel was first taught by his elder brother, Joseph, a portrait painter, who was occasionally employed by the House of Liechtenstein. In 1779/80, after attending the Viennese Academy of Fine Arts, Anton Hickel received portrait commissions from the courts of Munich and of Mannheim. In 1786/87 he was in Berne, and from there he moved on to Paris. At the French court he became a protégé of Queen Marie Antoinette and Princesse de Lamballe. At the outbreak of the Revolution he fled to London, where he painted a striking record of a debate in the Houses of Parliament, which included ninety-six life-size portraits. Between 1792 and 1796 Hickel regularly showed his portraits at the exhibitions mounted at the Royal Academy. In 1797 he moved to Hamburg, where he died the following year.

ANGELICA KAUFFMANN
Chur 1741–Rome 1807

Even as a child, Angelica Kauffmann had produced portraits that met with general admiration. In 1763 the young artist became acquainted with the work of the celebrated German art historian Johann Joachim Winckelmann, whose writings were largely responsible for the emerging vogue for Neoclassicism in art. Kauffmann's own portraits nonetheless always retained something of the lightness of Rococo painting. At the age of only twenty-three, Kauffmann was admitted to membership of the Accademia di San Luca in Rome. In 1766 she moved to London, which remained her base for fifteen years. Here, she became a founding member of the Royal Academy and enjoyed the most successful period of her career. In 1782 she returned to Rome, where she settled permanently. Here, she became a magnet for the intellectual élite of Europe as it passed through Rome on Grand Tours of the South. The geographical range of the commissions she received was correspondingly broad, including members of the English, Polish, Russian, Italian, and Austrian nobility.

JOHANN PETER KRAFFT
Hanau 1780–Vienna 1856

In 1799, after a period of study at the Drawing School established in Hanau by the Princes of Hesse, Krafft moved to the Viennese Academy of Fine Arts, where he trained as a portrait painter under Füger (qv). Between 1802 and 1804 he studied in the studio of Jacques-Louis David in Paris. Carried away by enthusiasm for the advent of a new type of history painting dedicated to the glorification of Napoleon, Krafft was subsequently influenced for some time by the work of two slightly older pupils of David, François Gérard and Antoine-Jean Gros. After his return to Vienna, Krafft obtained a stipend in 1808, which permitted him to study in Italy. In 1813 he was elected a member of the Viennese Academy, and in 1828 he was appointed Director of the Imperial Picture Gallery, then housed in Belvedere Palace. In his own history paintings Krafft replaced the pathos of the French works he had taken as a model with a more matter-of-fact, bourgeois mood. As a consciously patriotic form of art, his paintings were very much at the service of the new German understanding of history.

GIOVANNI BATTISTA LAMPI
Romeno 1751–Vienna 1830

Born in the South Tyrol (as Johann Baptist Lamp, a name he Italianised in 1781), Lampi trained as a history painter in Salzburg. It was only later, when he had worked also in Trent (now Trento, Italy) and in Klagenfurt, that he took up portrait painting, in due course achieving great success at many of the royal courts of Europe. He became the veritable society painter of his age. In 1783 Lampi settled in Vienna, though spending 1788 and 1797 at the courts, respectively, of Warsaw and St Petersburg. Thereafter he retuned to Vienna, where he mainly painted portraits commissioned by the Habsburgs and by members of the Austrian nobility, including the House of Liechtenstein. In 1798 Lampi was honoured with a hereditary title and in 1799 he was made an Honorary Citizen of Vienna.

FRANZ VON LENBACH
Schrobenhausen 1836–Munich 1904

In keeping with family tradition, Lenbach first trained as an architect. Through his brother, however, he found his way to painting. He was introduced to the practice of working en plein air by Johann Baptist Hofner, and he subsequently studied under Theodor von Piloty at the Munich Academy of Art. For Adolph Friedrich von Schack, Lenbach made copies in Rome of the works of the Old Masters and came to know the German painters Anselm Feuerbach and Hans von Marées and their Swiss-German colleague Arnold Böcklin. On account of his friendship with the Austrian painter Hans Makart, he spent much time in the late 1860s in Vienna. With the support of the composer Richard Wagner, of whom he painted several portraits, he here took on numerous portrait commissions. After returning to Munich he embarked, in 1878, on a portrait of Otto von Bismarck. This commission inaugurated Lenbach's career as an internationally acclaimed portrait painter, his sitters including many of the most celebrated men of the age. The results are notable for their distinctive 'Venetian' colouring, frequent use of historical costume, and altogether theatrical mise-en-scène. The Florentine Villa that Lenbach built in Munich in collaboration with Gabriel von Seidl is now a public museum, known as the Lenbachhaus. Lenbach was also involved in the founding of the Haus der Kunst and the Bayerisches Nationalmuseum, also both in Munich.

ANDREA LOCATELLI
Rome 1695–Rome 1741

Among the teachers of Locatelli was Monsù Alto (died around 1712), a specialist in seascapes, while his treatment of the human figure (in a style that was in future to typify the work of the bamboc-ciate) was influenced by Biagio Puccini. Through the architect Filippo Juvarra, Locatelli received an extremely important commission for two views of the unfinished Castello di Rivoli in Turin, in the execution of which he adapted Juvarra's designs (1723–25, Racconigi, Castello). Among Locatelli's patrons were Cardinals Alessandro Albani and Pietro Ottoboni and members of the Colonna family. Locatelli's style as a painter evolved from a realism that was still indebted to the late seventeenth century towards a much more idealising manner. He initially specialised in views of river and coastal landscapes, but he later developed these, through the addition of ruins, into Arcadian landscapes incorporating mythological episodes.

FRANZ XAVER MESSERSCHMIDT
Wiesensteig 1736 – Pressburg (now Bratislava) 1783

Messerschmidt trained at the Viennese Academy of Fine Arts, where he was probably taught by Jakob Schletterer and Balthasar Ferdinand Moll. Becoming a protégé of Martin van Meytens, Director of the Academy and painter to the Imperial Court, enabled Messerschmidt to obtain his first commissions from the same quarter. He produced portrait busts of both the Regent and his consort and the Emperor's heir and his consort and over-life-size statues of Maria Theresia and Franz I Stephan of Lorraine (Vienna, Österreichische Galerie Belvedere). These official portraits are typical examples of court art of the late Rococo period, although Messerschmidt was able to infuse his work with exceptional vitality. A trip to Rome in 1765 brought about a dramatic shift in the style of his work: his portrait of Franz von Scheyb was the first in a Neoclassical style to be made in Vienna. After his break with the Viennese Academy, in 1774, Messerschmidt's career took a turn for the worse. He left Vienna and thereafter led a very retiring life in Pressburg (now Bratislava). It was in this period that he made the studies of extreme facial expressions known to his contemporaries as 'character heads'.

JOSEPH NIGG
Vienna 1782–Vienna 1863

From 1800 to 1843 Nigg worked as a flower painter for the Viennese porcelain factory. From 1835 this post also involved holding classes in painting at the factory. A publication of 1818, marking the centenary of the founding of the factory, praised in particular Nigg's 'ability to work in the style of the masters of his speciality, such as Huysums, Ruysch, and others'. With the advent of the Biedermeier Era, flower painting became immensely popular and was also to be found on large porcelain plaques. A piece of this sort, thirty inches in height, was presented by Nigg, on behalf of the Viennese factory, at the London World Exhibition of 1851.

FRIEDRICH OELENHAINZ
Endingen 1745–Pfalzburg 1804

Friedrich Oelenhainz specialised in portrait painting. In 1766 he arrived in Vienna, together with his teacher, W. Beyer, and remained there until 1788. In 1776 Oelenhainz painted a series of portraits of the family of Prince Franz Josef I von Liechtenstein, which was set into a wall in the manor house at Eisgrub. Oelenhainz posed his sitters in a setting indicative of their status and, by means of delicate brushwork and predominantly pastel tones, evoked an atmosphere of great elegance. After his long period in Vienna, he did not again settle for long in any single city, the last decades of his career finding him, in turn, in Stuttgart, Zurich, Berne, Basle, Ulm, Rome, Karlsruhe, and Paris.

GIOVANNI PAOLO PANNINI
Piacenza 1691–Rome 1765

Pannini is above all known for his views of Rome, mostly centred on the chief architectural ruins of Antiquity. These *vedute*, which were greatly prized by travellers from across Europe passing through Rome, served not only as a form of souvenir but often offered fantastical combinations of the best-loved monuments. With his talent for the persuasive rendering of a sense of space, his precise drawing technique and cool colouring, and his deft integration of elegant figures, Pannini established a style that was to have many imitators. In their picturesque character, his *vedute* are distinct from those of Bellotto (qv), which made a virtue of topographical precision. Pannini testified to his artistic versatility through his designs for architecture and decorative programmes, as well as for the settings of elaborate festivities, where he was able to fall back on his first training, with a stage designer in his native Piacenza. Pannini was also in demand as a fresco painter and a portraitist. In the 1720s and 1730s he provided some decorative frescoes for the Papal court. His marriage to a Frenchwoman and his Professorship at the Académie de France in Rome ensured his influence, in due course, on numerous French artists, as well as on Robert (qv), who worked for a while in Pannini's studio.

GIUSEPPE PISANI
Carrara 1757–Modena 1839

After training as a sculptor at the Academy in Florence, Pisani worked until the 1790s in Rome, where he produced numerous busts and figures after models from Antiquity. From around 1797 he was employed in Milan as court sculptor to the Governor of Lombardy, Ferdinand Karl d'Este, and his consort, Maria Beatrix. In 1798, when these had been expelled from Lombardy by Napoleon, Pisani followed them to Vienna, where he was appointed court sculptor to Archduke Franz. Thanks to his busts of the Holy Roman Emperor Franz II (later Austrian Emperor Franz I), the Archduke Karl, and other members of the ruling House of Habsburg, Pisani swiftly made a name for himself. By 1807 he had established the largest sculpture studio in Vienna. Reputedly, from 1809, he took part in preparing the elaborate decorative programme for the apartments of Empress Maria Ludovica, née d'Este, in the Viennese Hofburg. Pisani is regarded as the most significant supporter and promoter of Johann Nepomuk Schaller, whom he trained in making sculptures after Classical models. Especially celebrated is the monument of 1821, commissioned by the Emperor, to Lieutenant Field Marshall Heinrich von Schmidt in Krems, which testifies to Pisani's enormous technical virtuosity. After the end of the Napoleonic Wars, Pisani returned to Italy. From 1814 he was *primo scultore* at the Academy in Modena, becoming Director of this institution in 1821. He continued to make sculpture for the Este family, including the tomb for Archbishop Karl Ambros d'Este in the Cathedral at Esztergom, Hungary, and a bust of Duke Francesco IV of Modena. Pisani's figures have been praised for their high technical quality, and his reliefs for their exceptionally complex and dazzling composition.

HERMANUS POSTHUMUS
East Frisian Islands *c.* 1513/14–Amsterdam 1588
Like van Heemskerck (*qv*), Posthumus trained in Utrecht in the studio of Jan van Scorel. Though primarily a painter, Posthumus was also on occasion active as an architect. In 1535 he and a painter colleague, Jan Cornelisz. Vermeyen, served as draughtsmen in the retinue of Emperor Karl V on his Tunisian campaign, which was recorded by both painters in numerous sketches. The *Landscape with Roman Ruins* in the Princely Collections, dated 1536 (though not discovered until 1980), strongly suggests that Posthumus was in Rome in that year. In 1536 he is also known to have collaborated on the decorations installed for the triumphal entry of Karl V into Rome. In 1540/42 Posthumus was employed by Wilhelm IV, Duke of Bavaria, to contribute to the decorations of his residence in Landshut, a scheme to which the artist made a substantial contribution. A number of artists from the Gonzaga court in Mantua also worked on this

decorative programme. The apparent influence of the work of Giulio Romano (court artist to the Gonzaga) on that of Posthumus at Landshut suggests that the latter must at some earlier date have spent some time in Mantua.

JOSEPH REBELL
Vienna 1787–Dresden 1828
Rebell may be regarded as the most important innovator of Viennese landscape painting in the early nineteenth century. In spite of his early death, his work proved extremely influential. His handling of light made an appreciable impact even on the work of Waldmüller (*qv*). Rebell initially trained as an architect at the Viennese Academy of Fine Arts, but then took up landscape painting. He was taught by Michael Wutky, who specialised in Italianate scenes with striking light effects, which may be assumed to explain Rebell's subsequent visits to Italy. In 1809 he travelled, via Switzerland, to northern Italy, and from 1815 to 1824 he worked in Rome, where he associated with the German artists' colony. It was here that his work came to the attention of Emperor Franz I, who acquired four of his pictures and in 1824 recalled him to Vienna to become Director of the Imperial Picture Gallery.

HYACINTHE RIGAUD
Perpignan 1659–Paris 1743
Rigaud was portraitist to the French royal family, in his long career recording no less than four generations of the House of Bourbon. With its images of the ruler and his courtiers, the aristocracy and the clergy, his work is a reflection of the age of Louis XIV. At an early stage his teachers in Perpignan had drawn his attention to the work of Anthony van Dyck, and it was from this that he evolved his own style of portraiture. Rigaud arrived in Paris in 1681 and, on the advice of Charles Lebrun, devoted himself exclusively to portrait painting. In 1688 he inaugurated his career as court painter with the widely admired *Portrait of Duke Philippe of Orléans*, the king's brother. In 1694 he painted his first portrait of the Sun King. Rigaud was regarded as

unequalled in his ability to meet the needs of his sitters for a distinguished appearance and the affirmation of social status. It was for this reason that he also received numerous portrait commissions from foreign aristocrats who were passing through the French capital. His biographer, Joseph Roman, counted portrait sittings with six kings, thirty-six princes, twenty-one marshals, eighteen dukes, and sixty-four cardinals, archbishops, and bishops.

HUBERT ROBERT
Paris 1733–Paris 1808
Robert's contemporaries valued him above all as a painter of ruins and of architecture, but he also painted landscapes and was a keen observer of human life in both rural and urban settings. After initially training in the studio of the sculptor Michel-Ange Slodtz, Robert lived in Rome and Naples from 1754 to 1765. In Paris, meanwhile, his reputation grew rapidly. In 1778 he was appointed 'draughtsman of the king's gardens' and became a member of the Curatorial Committee convened to oversee the king's collections. In the years of the French Revolution, the Directoire, and the Empire Robert became one of the founders of the Musée du Louvre. This task also found its reflection in his work as a painter, for he repeatedly painted the Grande Galerie of the Louvre, most strikingly in the guise of a ruin. Robert's work was notable, on the one hand, for its commitment to topographical accuracy and, on the other, for the alienation of the observed and its reinterpretation in the spirit of the fantastical *capriccio*.

MASSIMILIANO SOLDANI BENZI
Florence 1656–Montevarchi 1740
On account of his birth in Florence, Soldani Benzi enjoyed the patronage of the Medici princes. After attending the drawing school they had founded in that city, he was sent by Grand Duke Cosimo III de' Medici to Rome, then after four years to Paris, in order to train as a medallist. During this time his portrait medallions attracted enormous attention, including that of Queen Christina of Sweden and King Louis XIV of France. Soldani Benzi nonetheless returned to Florence, where he was appointed Director of the Grand Ducal Mint. In the late seventeenth century Soldani Benzi was regarded as the best bronze caster in Europe. He maintained a workshop in the Uffizi in Florence and it was here that he received a visit from Prince Karl Eusebius von Liechtenstein. Although his reliefs, busts, and figures were often made in imitation of the art of Antiquity, he also produced works of his own devising. For Prince Johann Adam I von Liechtenstein Soldani Benzi made copies of masterpieces in the Florentine collections, of the sculpture of Antiquity, and of the work of Michelangelo and Giambologna.

PETER EDUARD STRÖHLING
Düsseldorf 1768–London after 1826
Ströhling embarked on his career as an artist in Russia, where his first important patrons were the Empress Catherine the Great and her son, Paul I. After his return to western Europe, he worked in Italy, France, and Austria, where he was much admired as a portraitist and a history painter. In the late 1790s he received portrait commissions not only from the Prince of Wales (later King George IV), but also from Prince Alois I von Liechtenstein and his wife, Princess Karoline von Liechtenstein, née Countess of Manderscheit. British connoisseurs would seem to have been particularly drawn to the refined and painstaking quality of his paintings, which distinguished them from contemporary work by British artists, although his output was in every other respect characteristic of portrait painting in his era.

PIETRO TENERANI
Torano, Massa e Carrara 1798–Rome 1869
Tenerani initially trained under Lorenzo Bartolini and Pietro Marchetti in Carrara. In 1814 he received a stipend enabling him to study in Rome, where he came to know Canova (qv) and Bertel Thorvaldsen, working for a time in the latter's studio. Tenerani first achieved international acclaim with his figure of Psyche (1817, Florence, Palazzo Pitti). After Thorvaldsen had left Rome, in 1838, Tenerani inherited his position as the most important sculptor working in that city. Among his most celebrated works was Cupid Pulling a Thorn out of the Foot of Venus and the large relief of the Deposition (Laternao, San Giovanni). Tenerani freed himself from the aesthetic tradition of Neoclassicism in favour of Romanticism, and in particular Italian Purismo, signing its manifesto in 1843. This Italian equivalent to the German Nazarene movement found its ideal in the early work of Raphael with its affirmation of the importance of drawing and its insistence on idealism. As President of the Accademia di San Luca and Director of both the Capitoline Museums and the Vatican Collections in Rome, Tenerani played a central role in the cultural life of mid-nineteenth-century Rome.

ELISABETH VIGÉE-LEBRUN
Paris 1755–Paris 1842
As one of the most admired portrait painters of her day, Vigée-Lebrun has left us a record of the elegance and the vital consciousness of the late eighteenth century. She was first trained by her father, Louis Vigée, but was thereafter largely self-taught, above all through making copies of works by Peter Paul Rubens, Anthony van Dyck, and Jean-Baptiste Greuze. She became the favourite painter of Marie Antoinette and produced over twenty portraits of the French Queen and her children. Vigée-Lebrun's Parisian salon was a magnet for the French aristocracy and her portraits its mirror. In 1789, at the outbreak of the French Revolution, Vigée-Lebrun moved to Italy. In 1793–94 she visited Vienna and later Berlin and St Petersburg. In 1802 she returned to France. Her memoirs provide a detailed record of the life of a woman artist at the eighteenth-century French court.

FERDINAND GEORG WALDMÜLLER
Vienna 1793–Hinterbrühl, near Vienna 1865
Starting out as a stage painter and a copyist, Waldmüller found his own way as an artist relatively late in life, eventually settling on portrait and genre painting and, above all, landscape painting. Here, however, he eschewed the fantastical, highly wrought composition, complete with staffage. He insisted on truthfulness in the rendering of the natural world, and was one of the first painters to work en plein air. He had a unique manner of painting bright sunlight, which bestows clarity and serenity on his landscapes. In 1830 Waldmüller was appointed Curator of the Gallery of the Viennese Academy of Fine Arts. Pugnacious and unyielding, he brought about a reform of teaching at this institution and advocated the practice of the direct observation of nature. On account of his uncompromising stance, he was forced into retirement and remained isolated within the Viennese art world.

FRANZ ANTON ZAUNER
Unterfalpetan 1746–Vienna 1822
Zauner was one of the most influential sculptors of
Austrian Neoclassicism. His stylistic development
was determined by his training under Jakob Schletterer and Wilhelm Bayer. He owed his first official
commission in Vienna, in 1775, to Prince Wenzel
Anton Kaunitz-Rietburg: the allegorical figures of
the River Danube and the River Enns for the fountains in the cour d'honneur at the palace at
Schönbrunn, which still clearly reveal the influence
of Georg Raffael Donner. Zauner spent the years
1776–81 in Rome. Here, under the influence of
the writings of the German art historian Johann
Joachim Winkelmann, he began to favour a Neoclassicism that was more rigorous and more
strongly indebted to models of Antiquity. On returning to Vienna he pursued his career with a Professorship, from 1782, at the Academy of Fine Arts,
where he served as Director from 1806 to 1815.
Zauner provided sculpture for the chief façade of
the Viennese palace of Count Fries, on Josefsplatz,
one of the few rigorously Neoclassical palaces to
be found in the city. Zauner also achieved great
success with tomb sculpture and as a portraitist.
His masterpiece, the equestrian monument to
Josef II (made in 1780–1806), was also the first
large sculpture of its type to be erected in Vienna.
The success of this work helped to revive the
Austrian tradition of bronze casting, which had for
some time been eclipsed by casting in lead.

PHOTOGRAPHIC ACKNOWLEDGEMENTS

The illustrations come from the collections of
the Princes of Liechtenstein in Vaduz
with the exception of:
Moravian Regional Archives, Brno: pp. 25 (left),
33 (bottom)
Sammlung Schönborn-Buchheim:
pp. 48, 49
Private Collection, Vienna: pp. 52 (left), 106
Esterházy-Privatstiftung, Eisenstadt: p. 75
The Royal Collection, © 2004 Her Majesty Queen
Elizabeth II: p. 53
Galleria degli Uffizi, Tribuna, Florence: p. 54 (left)
Staatliche Museen, Neue Galerie, Kassel: p. 101
Graphische Sammlung Albertina, Vienna:
p. 33 (top)

First published on the occasion of the exhibition 'Klassizismus und Biedermeier', held at the LIECHTENSTEIN MUSEUM, Vienna, 29 March – 7 November 2004.

CONCEPT AND DESIGN Johann Kräftner

PUBLICITY Alexandra Hanzl

REGISTRAR, FIT-UP Michael Schweller

RESTORATION Robert Wald, Helga Musner, Ruth Klebel, Tanja Neuhorn

PICTURE EDITOR Michael Schweller

PHOTOGRAPHS Atelier Kräftner, Vienna; image industry, Brno; Photostudio Preute, Vaduz; Collection of the Prince of Liechtenstein, Vaduz

REPRO Alexander Dillinger and Christian Ziegler at Grasl Druck & Neue Medien, A-2540 Bad Vöslau, Austria

EDITORIAL AND ACADEMIC ASSISTANT
Stefan Körner

The Library of Congress Cataloguing-in-Publication data is available; British Library Cataloguing-in-Publication Data: a catalogue record for this book is available from the British Library; Deutsche Bibliothek holds a record of this publication in the Deutsche Nationalbibliografie; detailed bibliographical data can be found under: http://dnb.ddb.de

Front cover: Friedrich von Amerling, *Lost in her Dreams*, c. 1835 (detail; cf. p. 156)
Back cover: Giovanni Paolo Pannini, *The Interior of the Pantheon in Rome*, 1735 (detail; cf. p. 59)
pp. 8–9: Jakob Alt, *View of the Amphitheatre at Maria Enzersdorf by Joseph Hardtmuth* (built 1810–11), watercolour, 1913 (detail)
p. 10: Joseph Höger, *Interior of the Grenzschloss by Franz Engel* (built 1826–27) with a view of Bischofswart Pond, watercolour, 1839
pp. 40–41: Marcantonio Franceschini, *Diana and Actaeon*, 1692/98 (detail; cf. p. 51)
pp. 70–71: Elisabeth Vigée-Lebrun, *Portrait of Princess Karoline von Liechtenstein, née Countess of Manderscheit (1768–1831), as Iris*, 1793 (detail; cf. p. 94)
pp. 114–15: Friedrich von Amerling, *Study of the Head of a Bearded Man* (detail; cf. p. 150)
pp. 176–77: Friedrich Oelenhainz, *Portrait of the Future Prince Alois I von Liechtenstein (1759–1805)*, 1776 (detail; cf. p. 90)

Prestel books are available worldwide. Please contact your nearest bookseller or one of the following Prestel offices for information concerning your local distributor:

Prestel Verlag
Königinstrasse 9, 80539 Munich
Tel. +49 (89) 38 17 09-0
Fax +49 (89) 38 17 09-35

Prestel Publishing Ltd.
4 Bloomsbury Place, London WC1A 2QA
Tel. +44 (20) 7323-5004
Fax +44 (20) 7636-8004

Prestel Publishing
900 Broadway, Suite 603, New York, NY 10003
Tel. +1 (212) 995-2720
Fax +1 (212) 995-2733

www.prestel.com

PROJEKT CO-ORDINATION Victoria Salley

EDITING Michele Schons

TRANSLATION Elizabeth Clegg

DESIGN WIEN NORD PILZ Werbeagentur, Vienna and Meike Sellier, Munich

PRODUCTION AND TYPESETTING Meike Sellier

REPRO, PRINTING AND BINDING
Grasl Druck & Neue Medien, A-2540 Bad Vöslau, Austria

Printed in Austria on acid-free paper

ISBN 3-7913-3146-9 (English edition)
ISBN 3-7913-3145-0 (German edition)
ISBN 3-7913-3147-7 (Italian edition)